This Big Cat Coloring Book is in loving dedication of Cesar the Lion

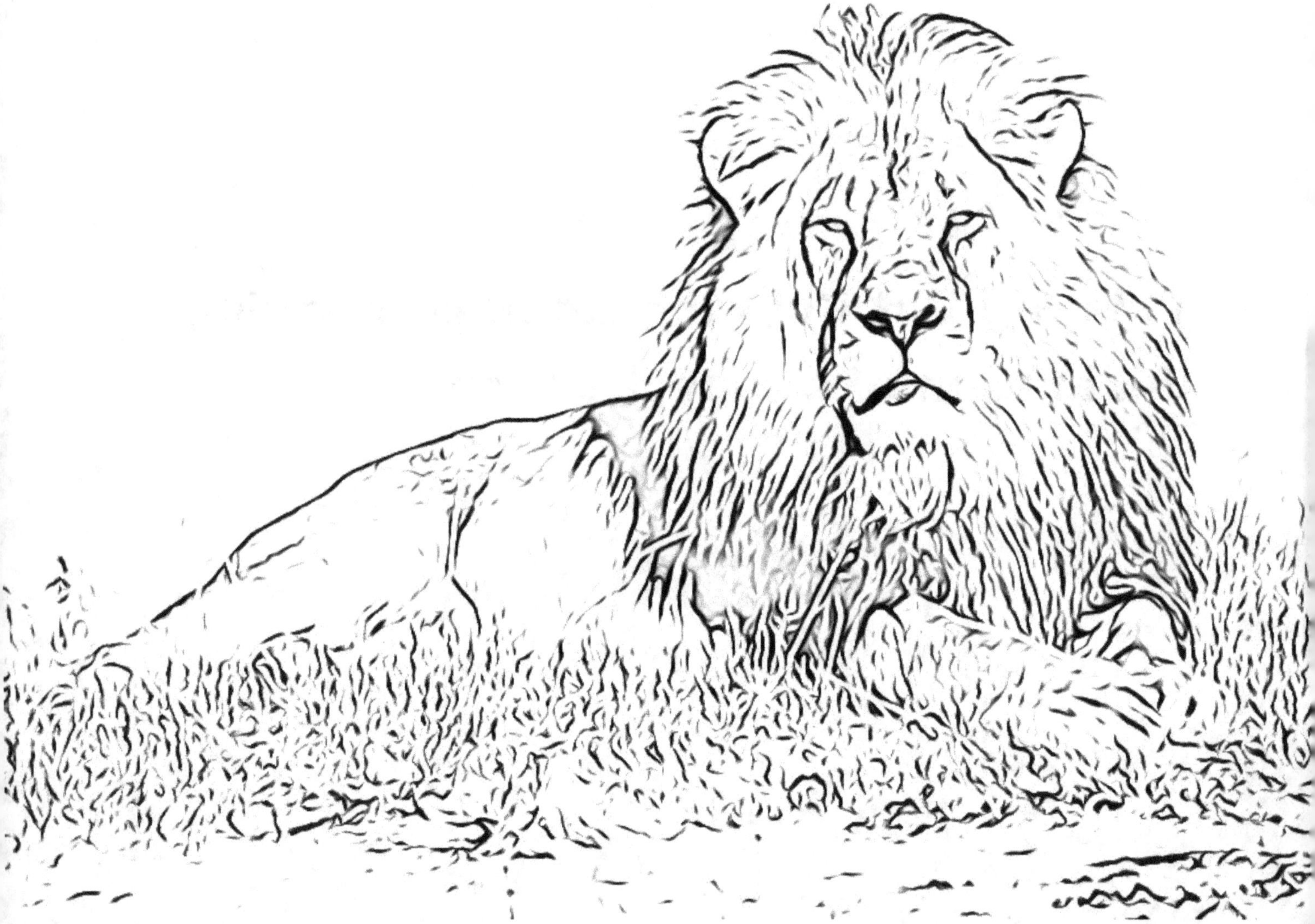

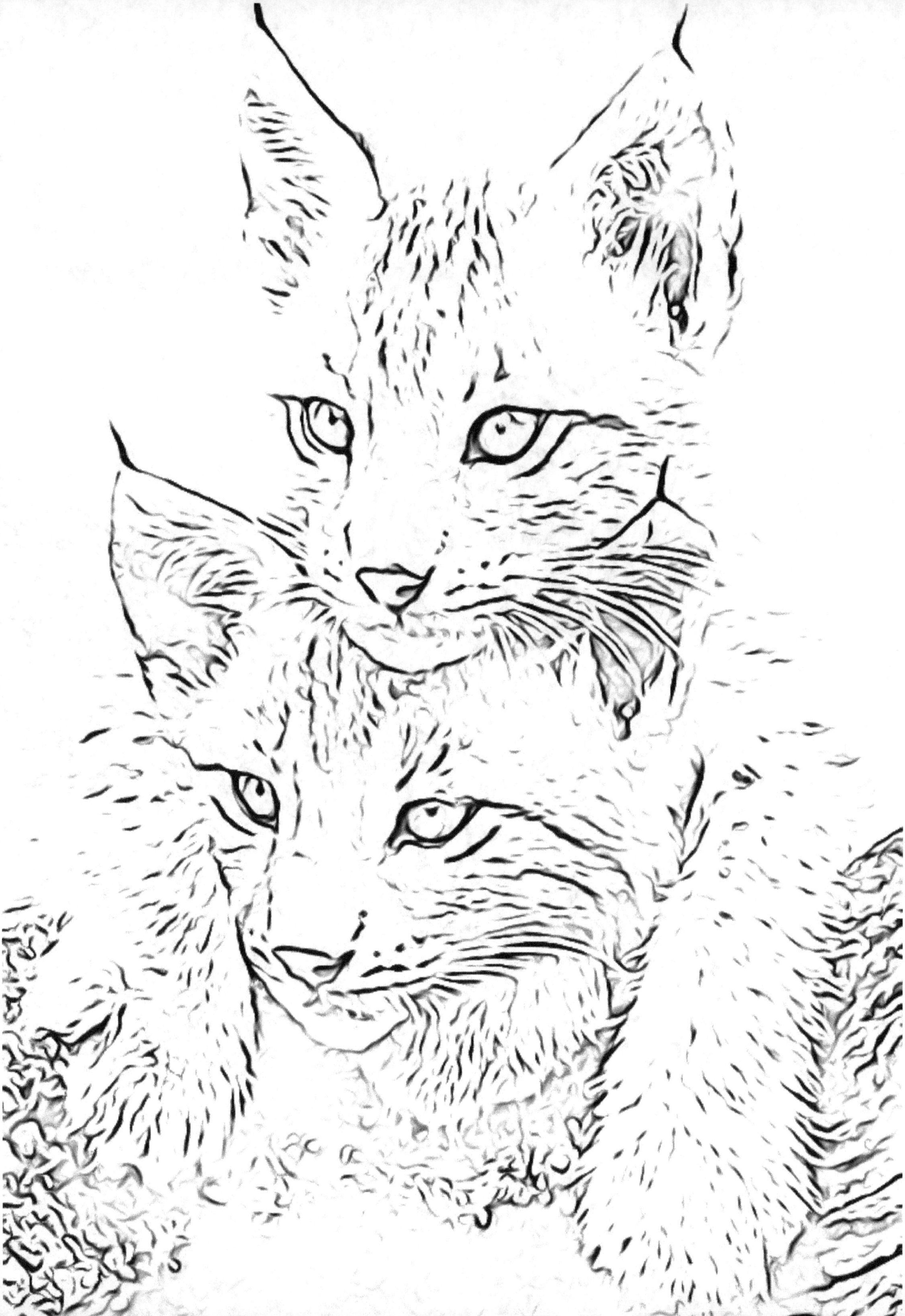

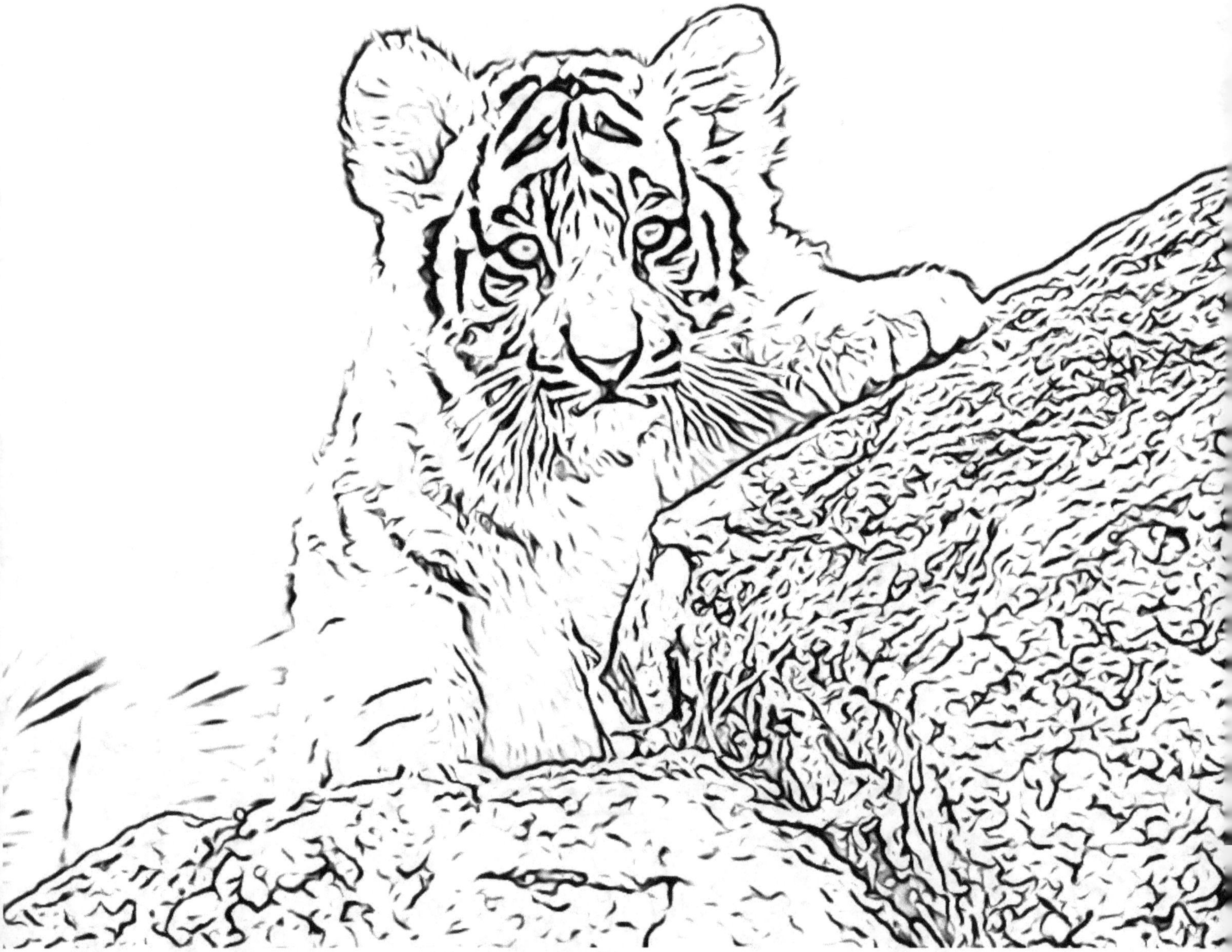

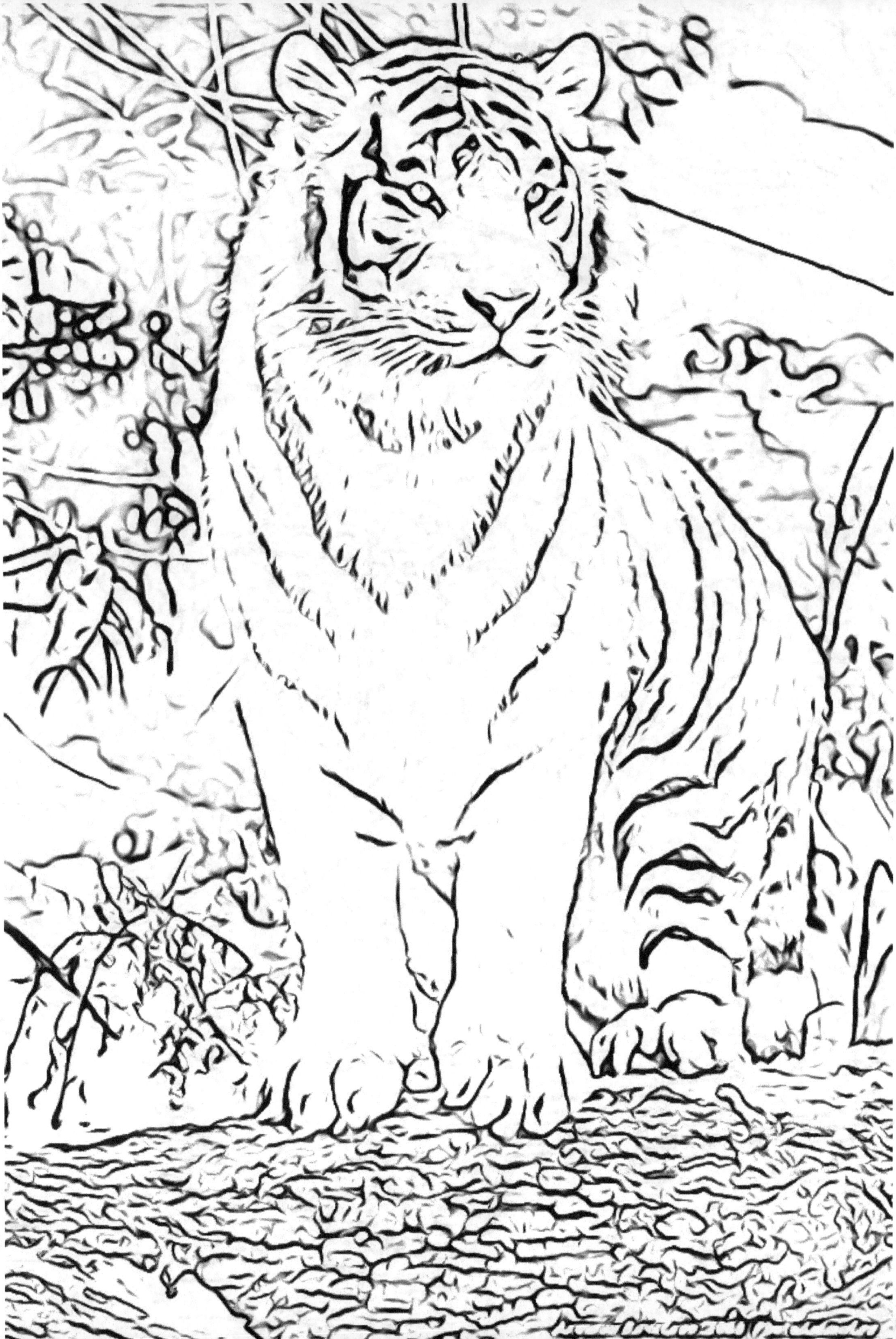

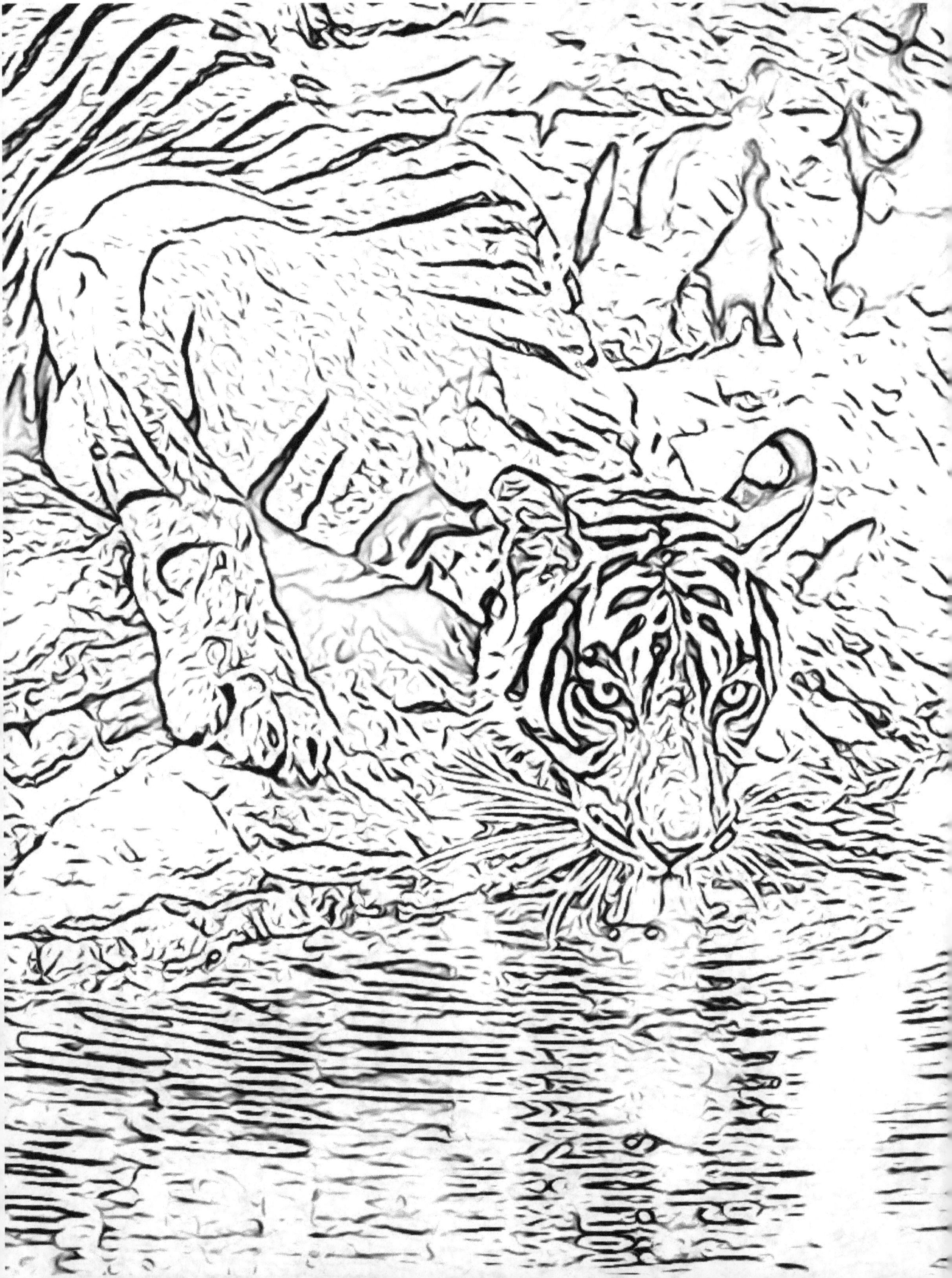

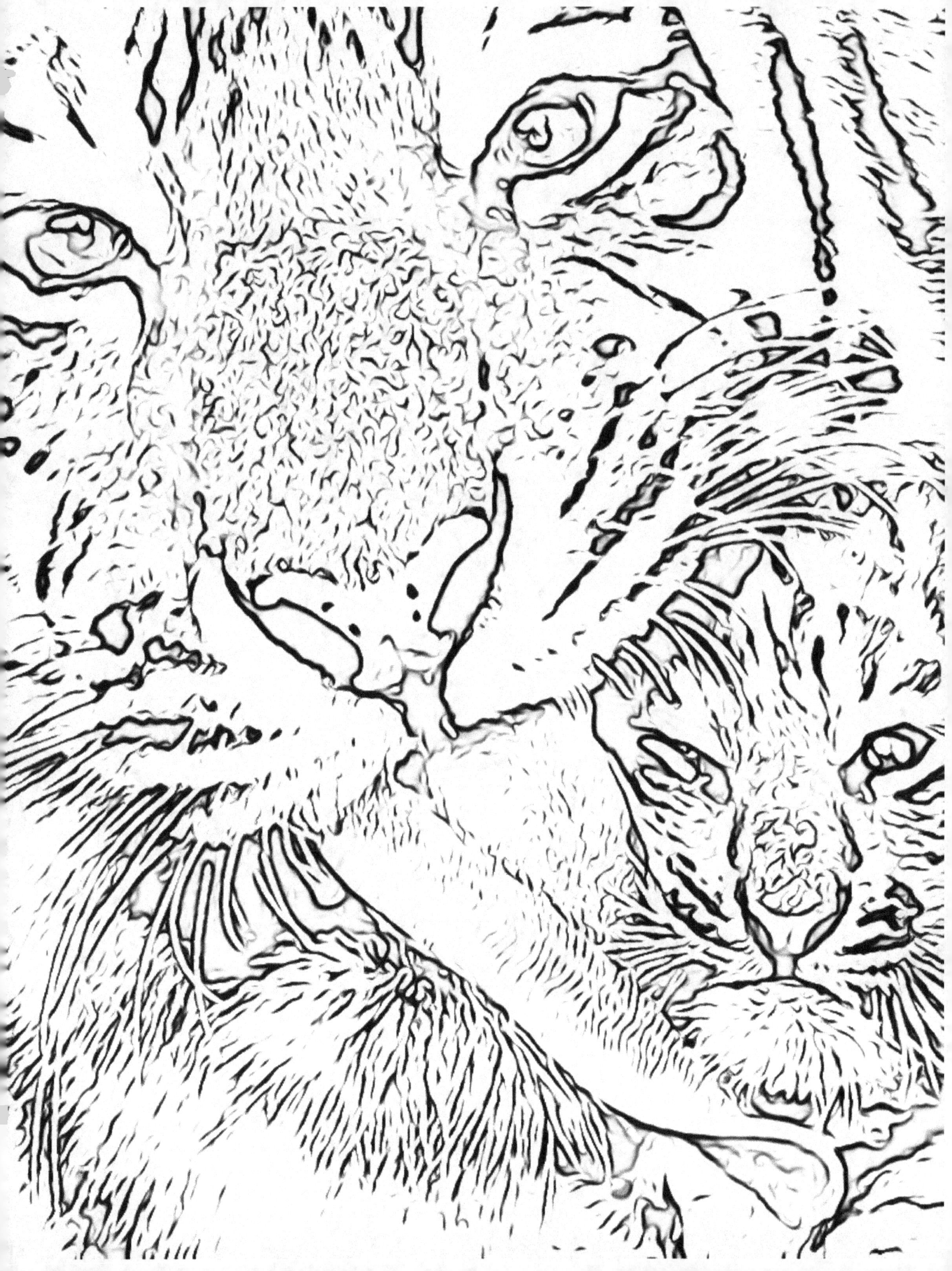

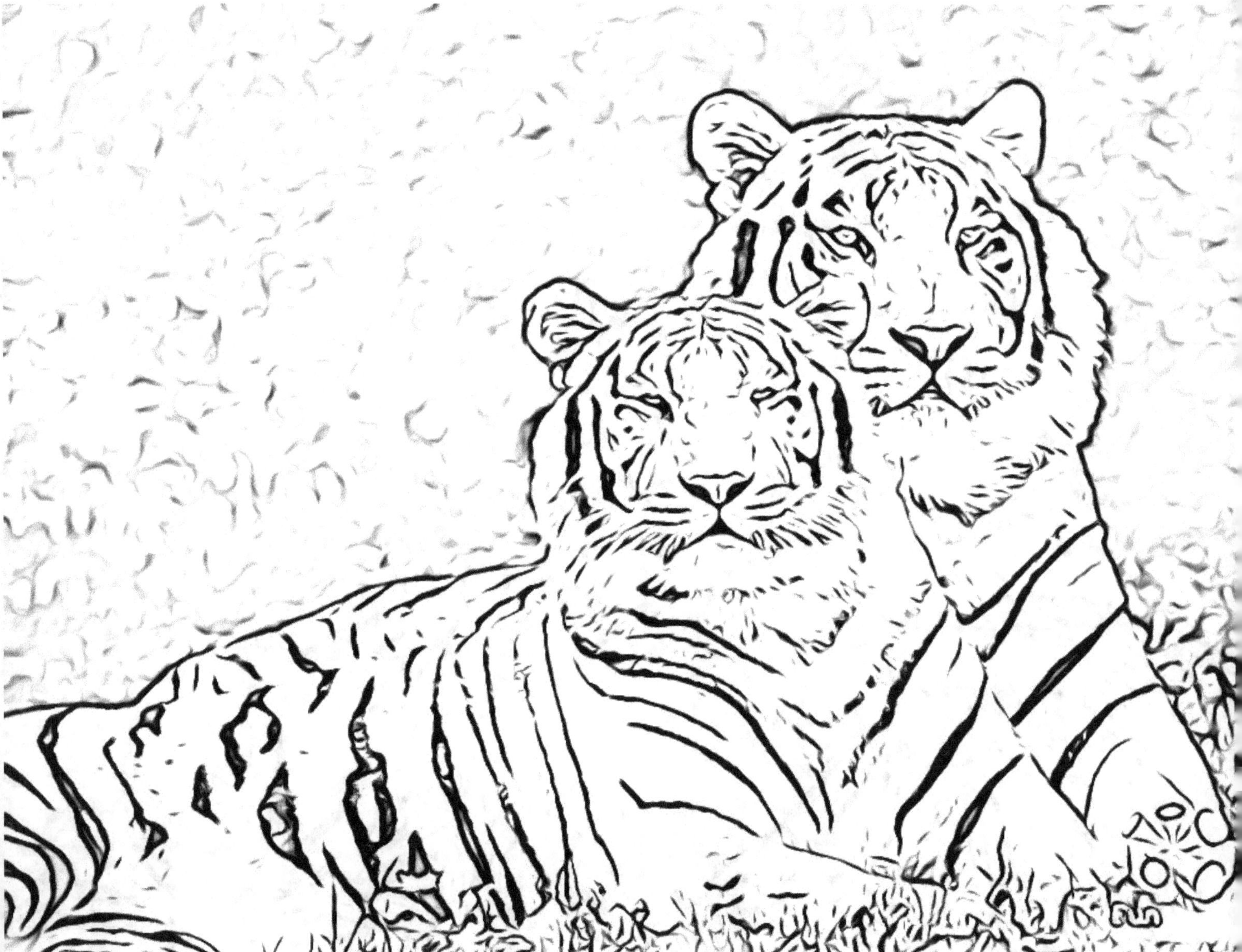

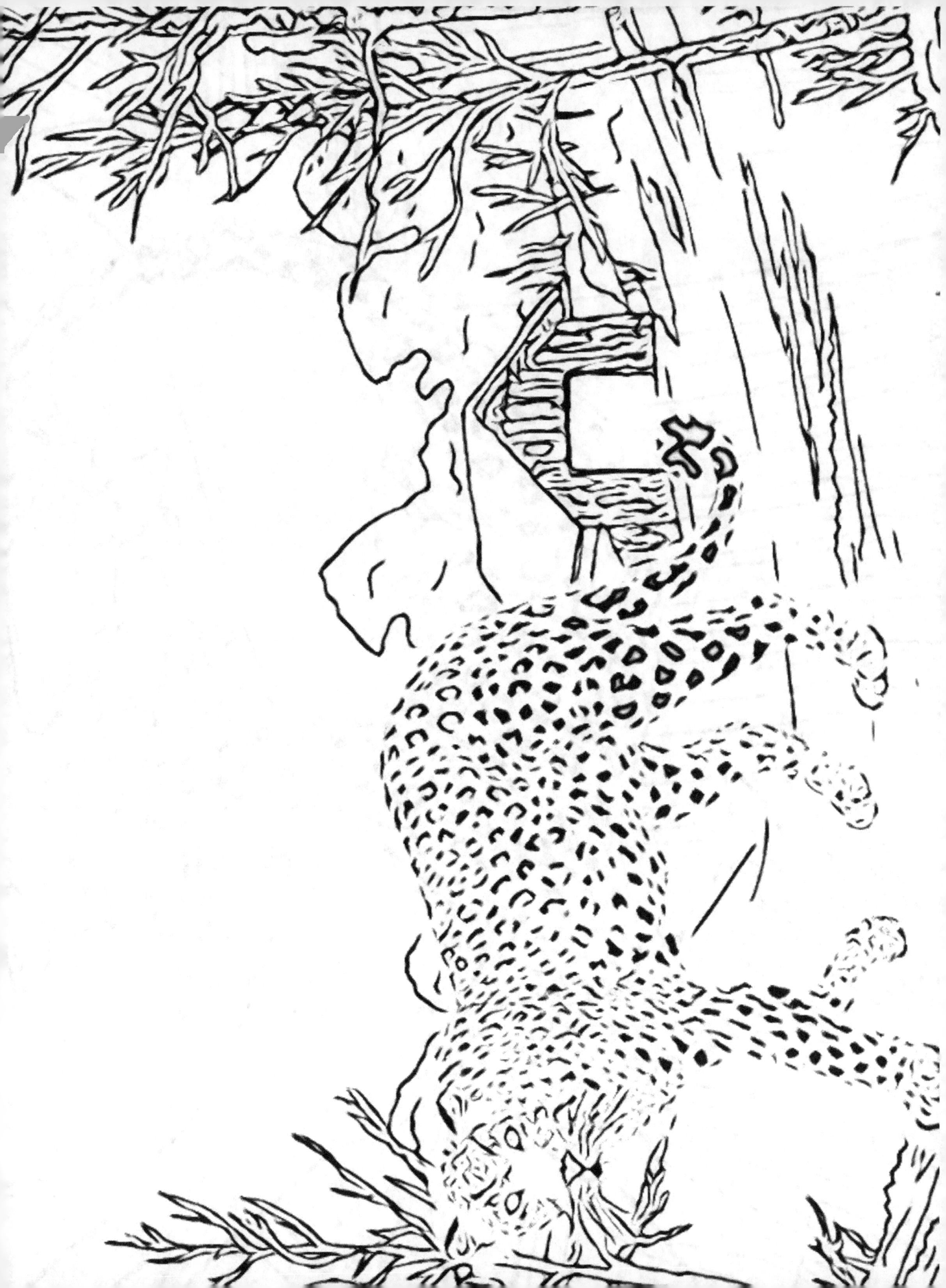

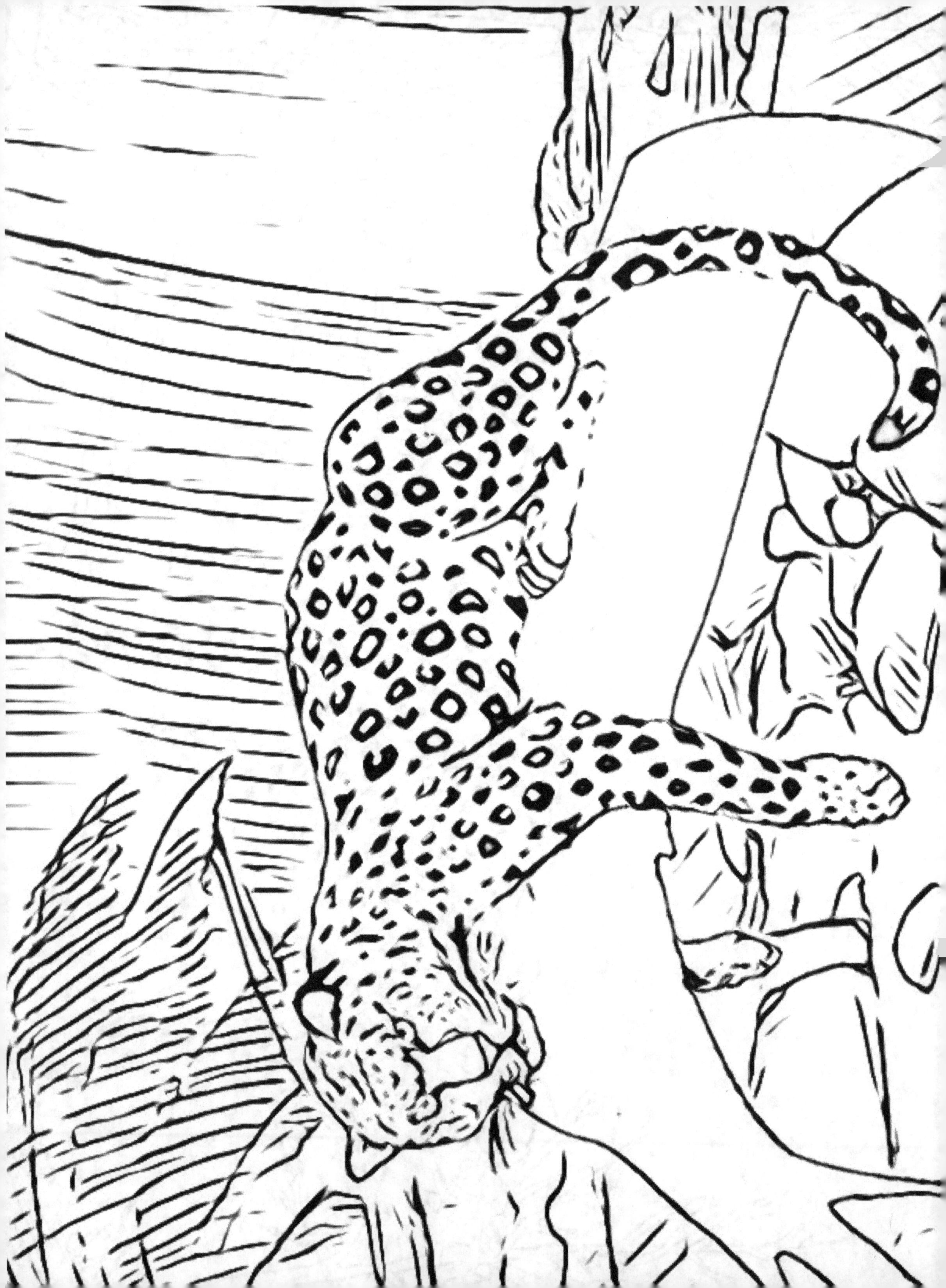

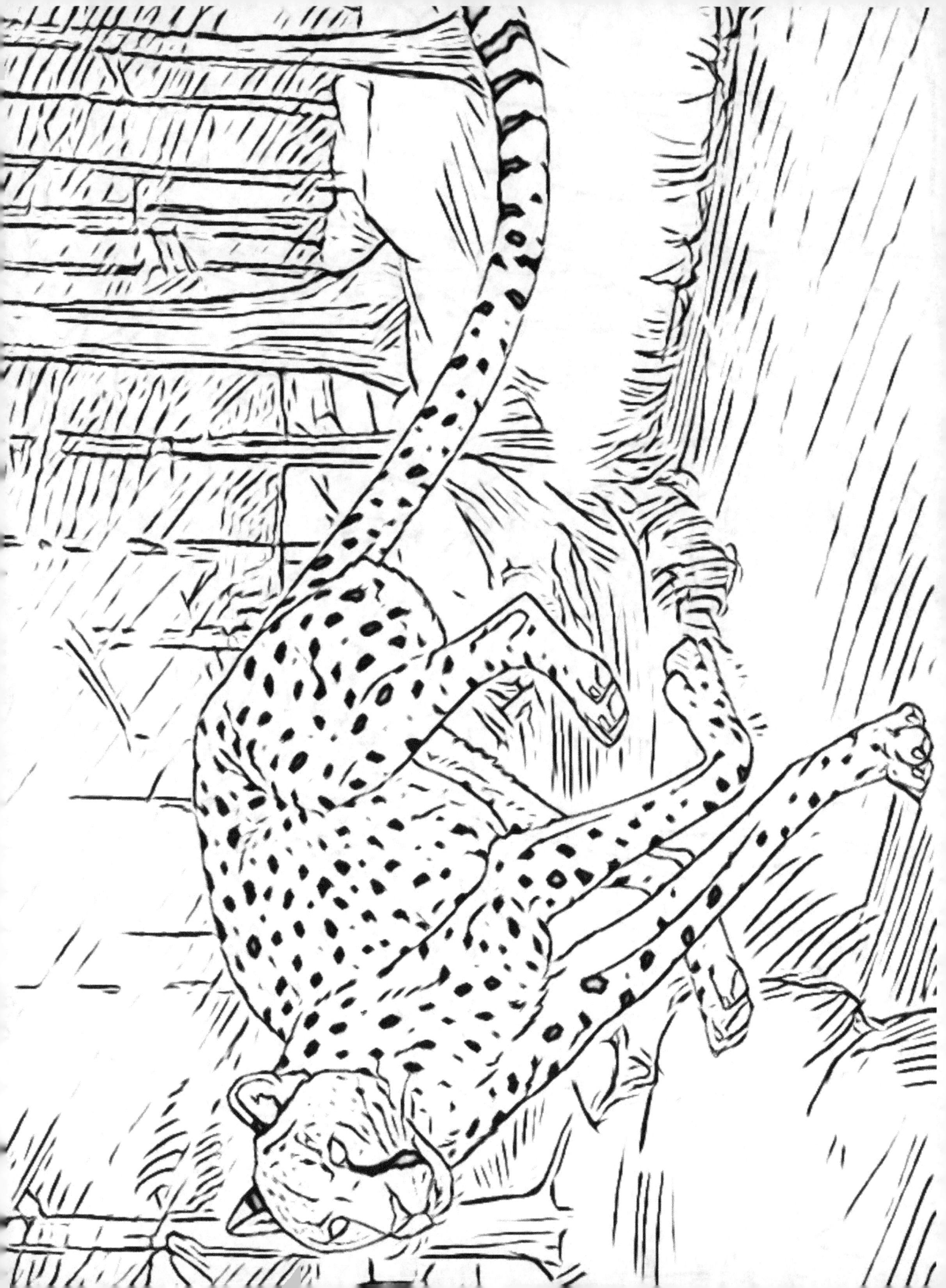

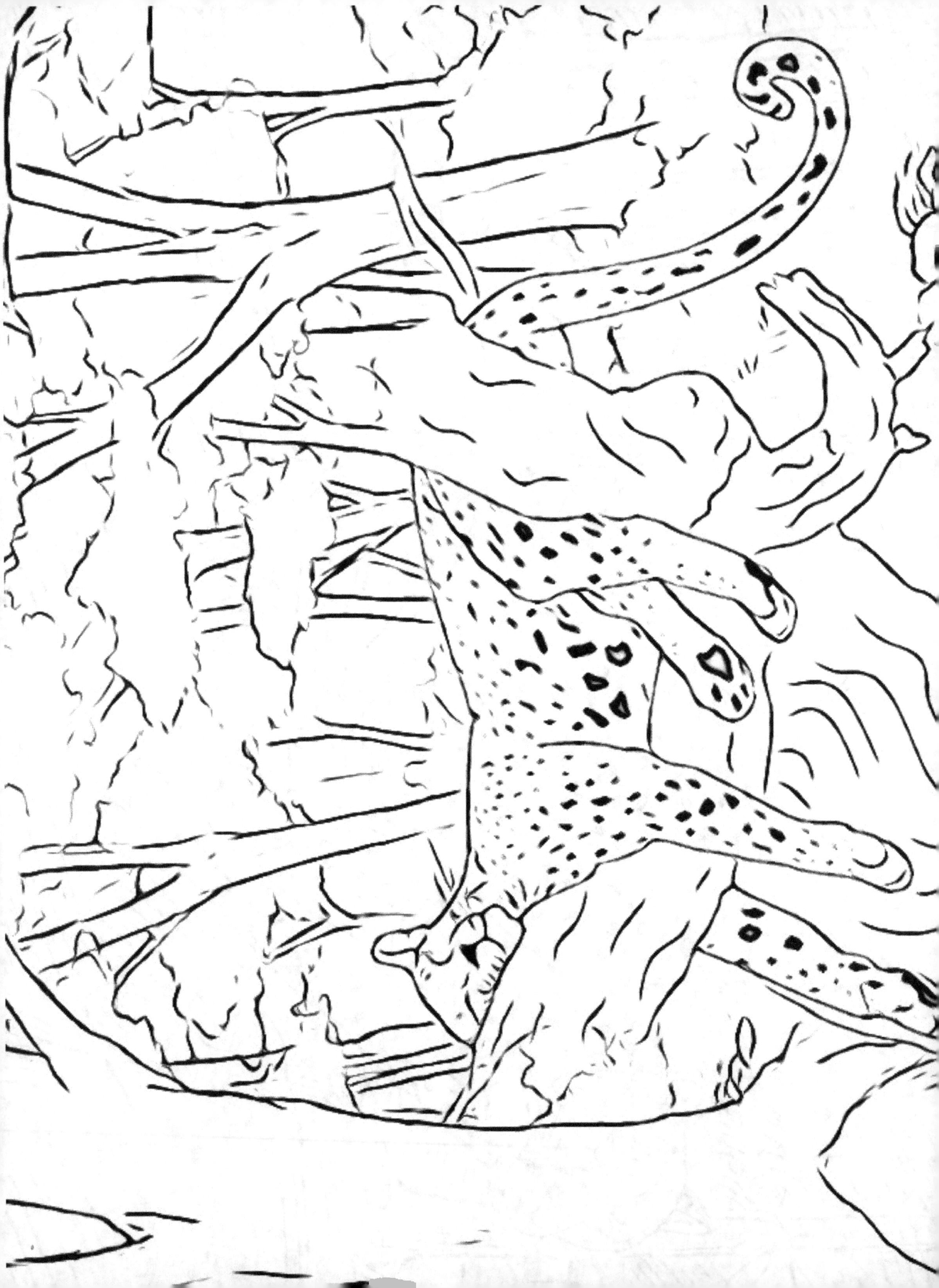

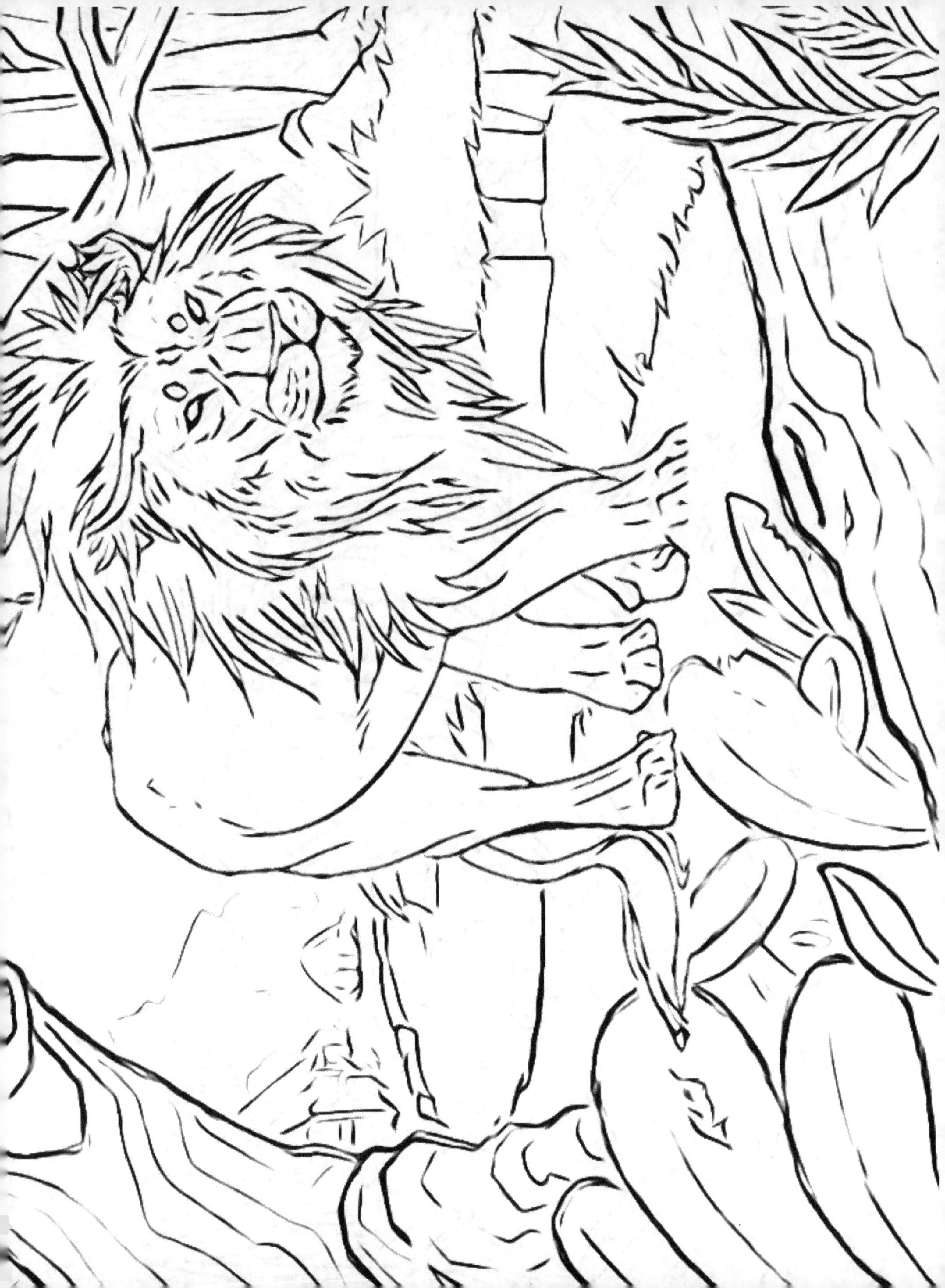

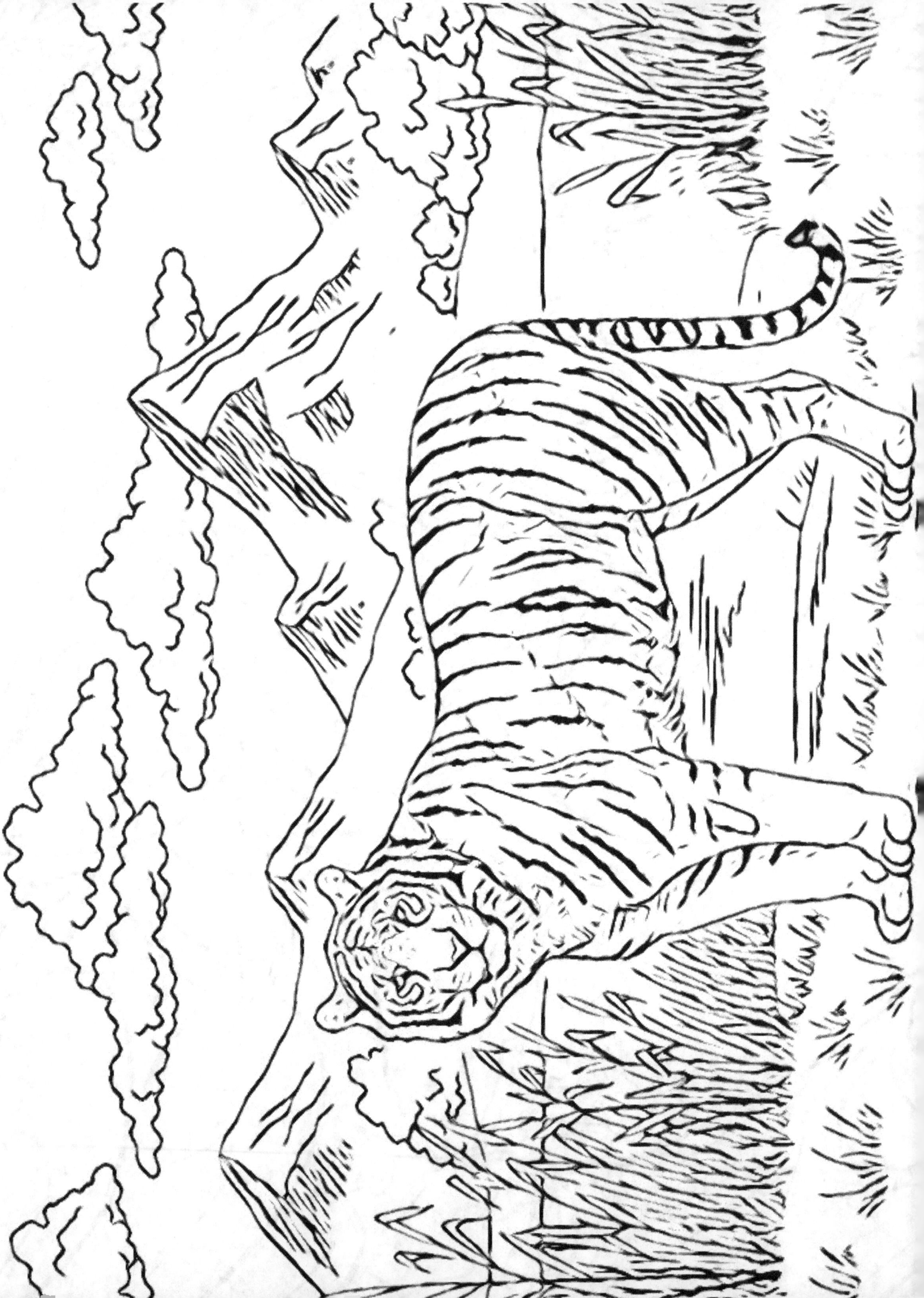

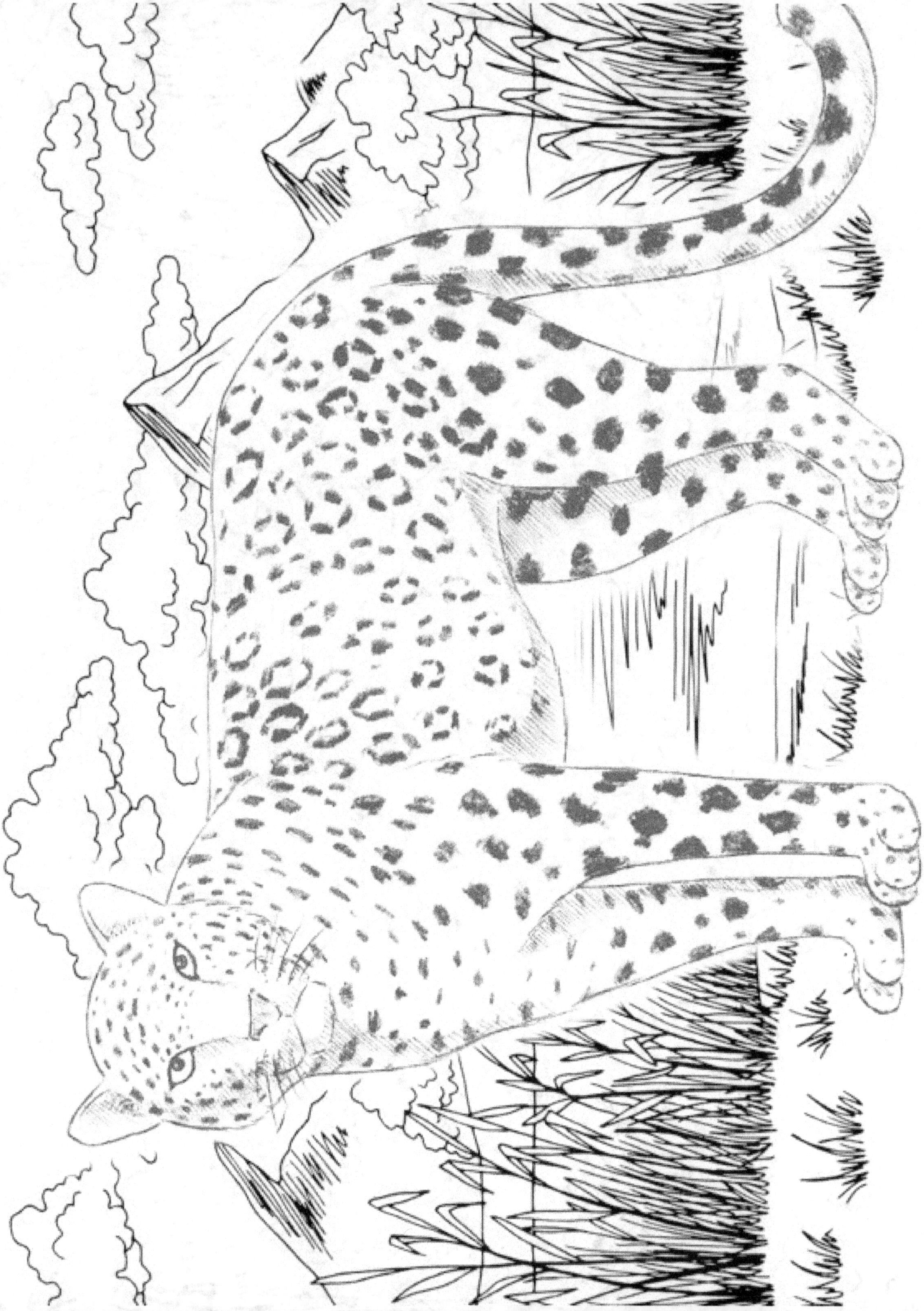

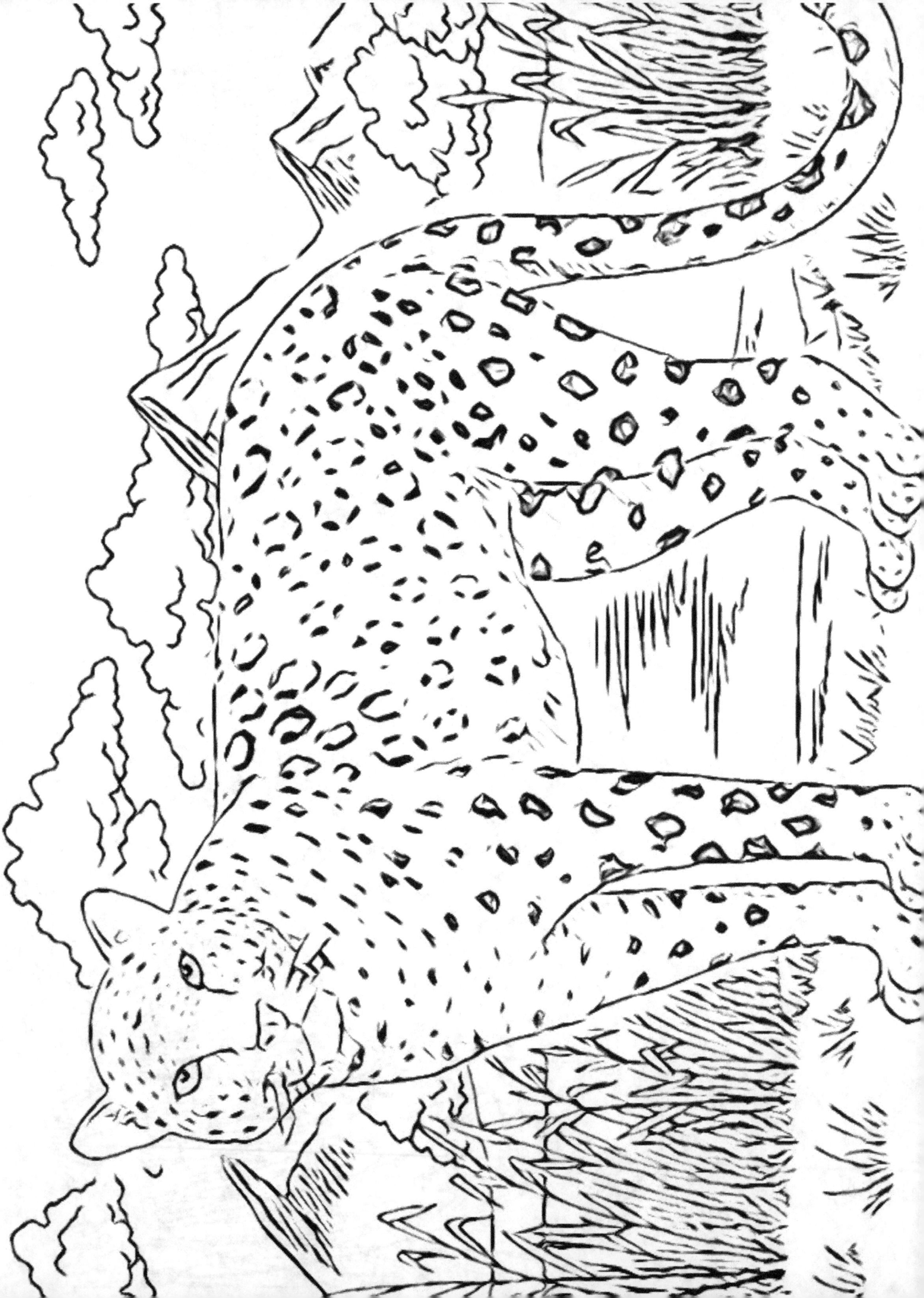

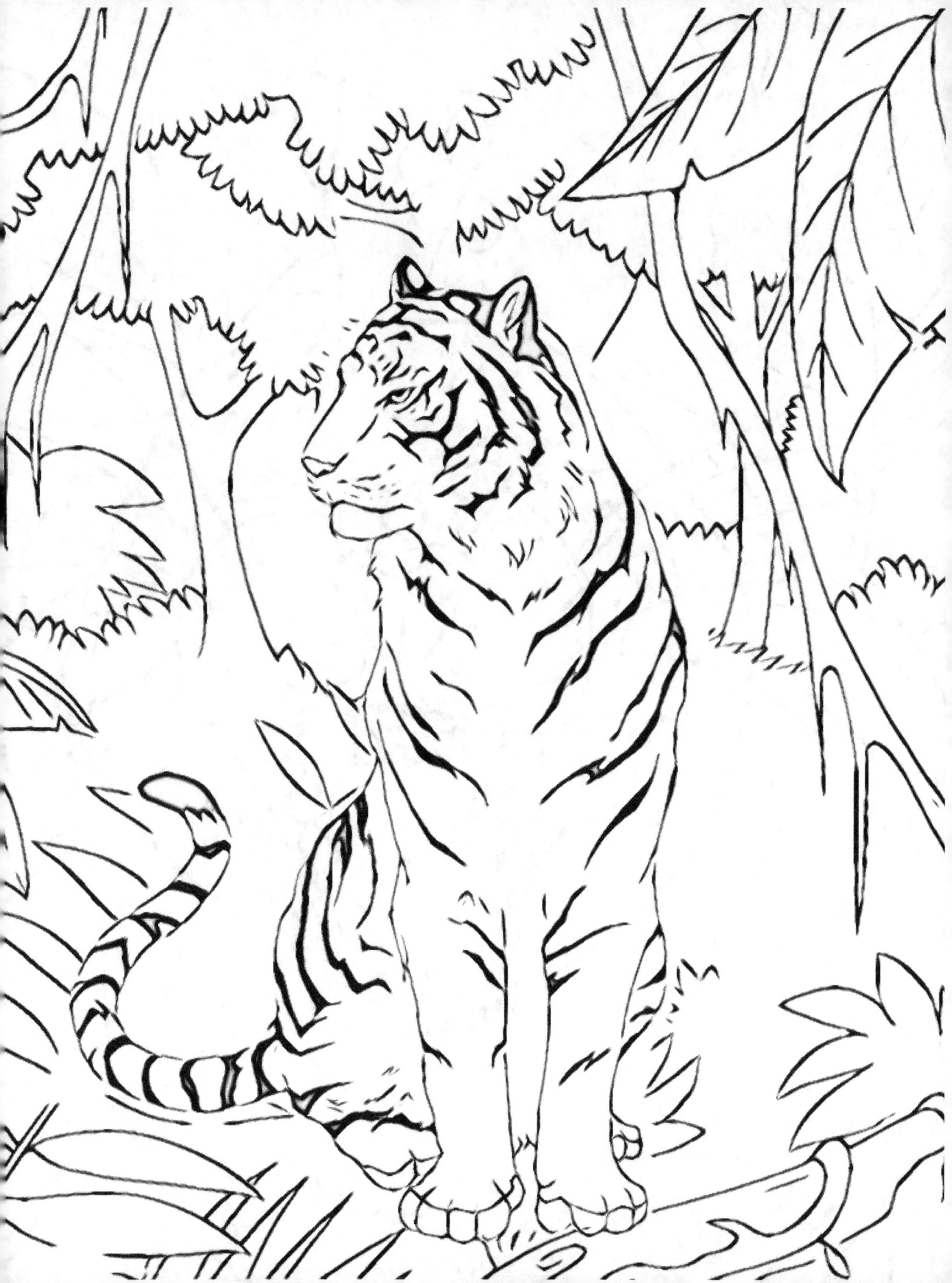

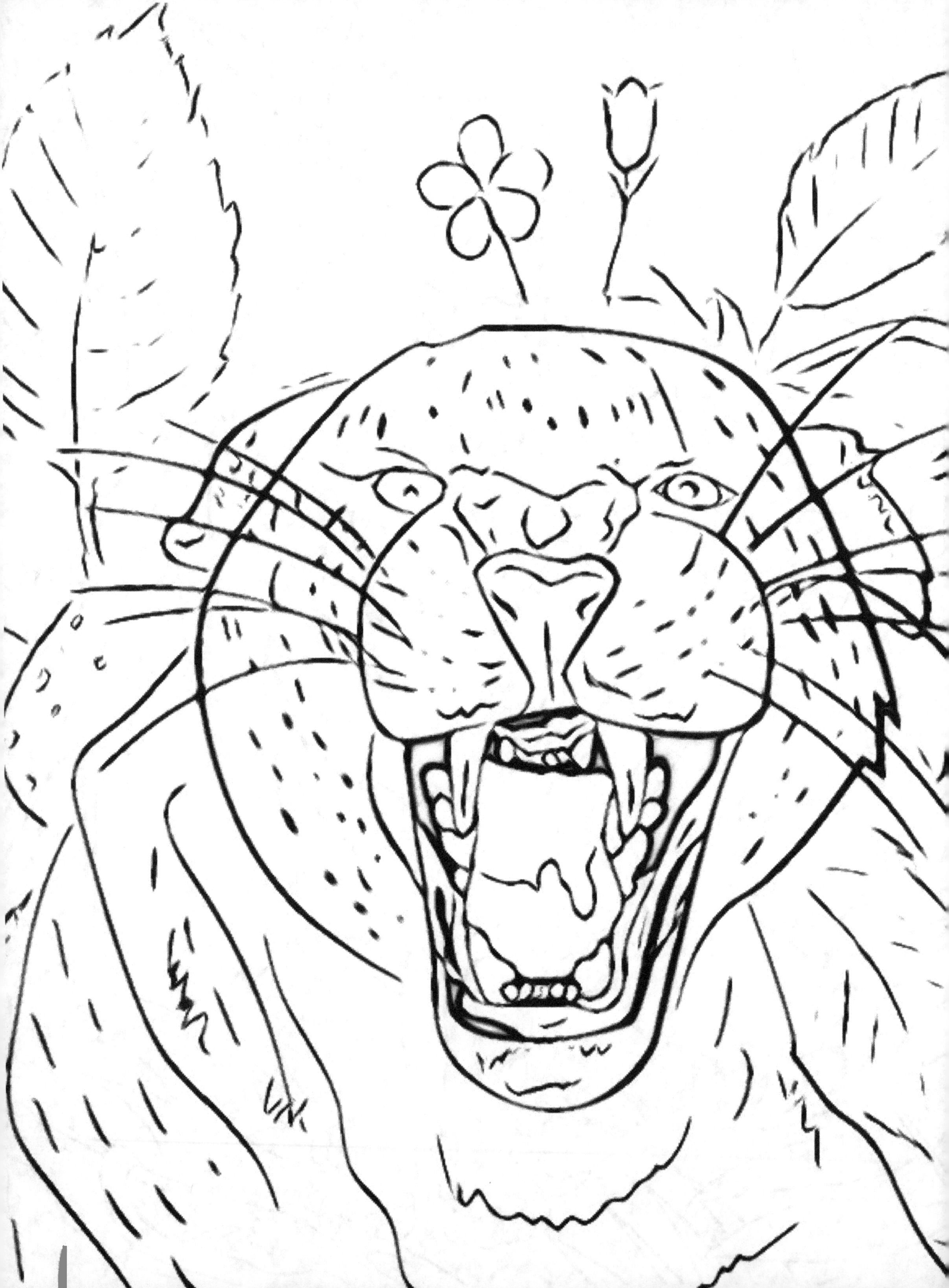

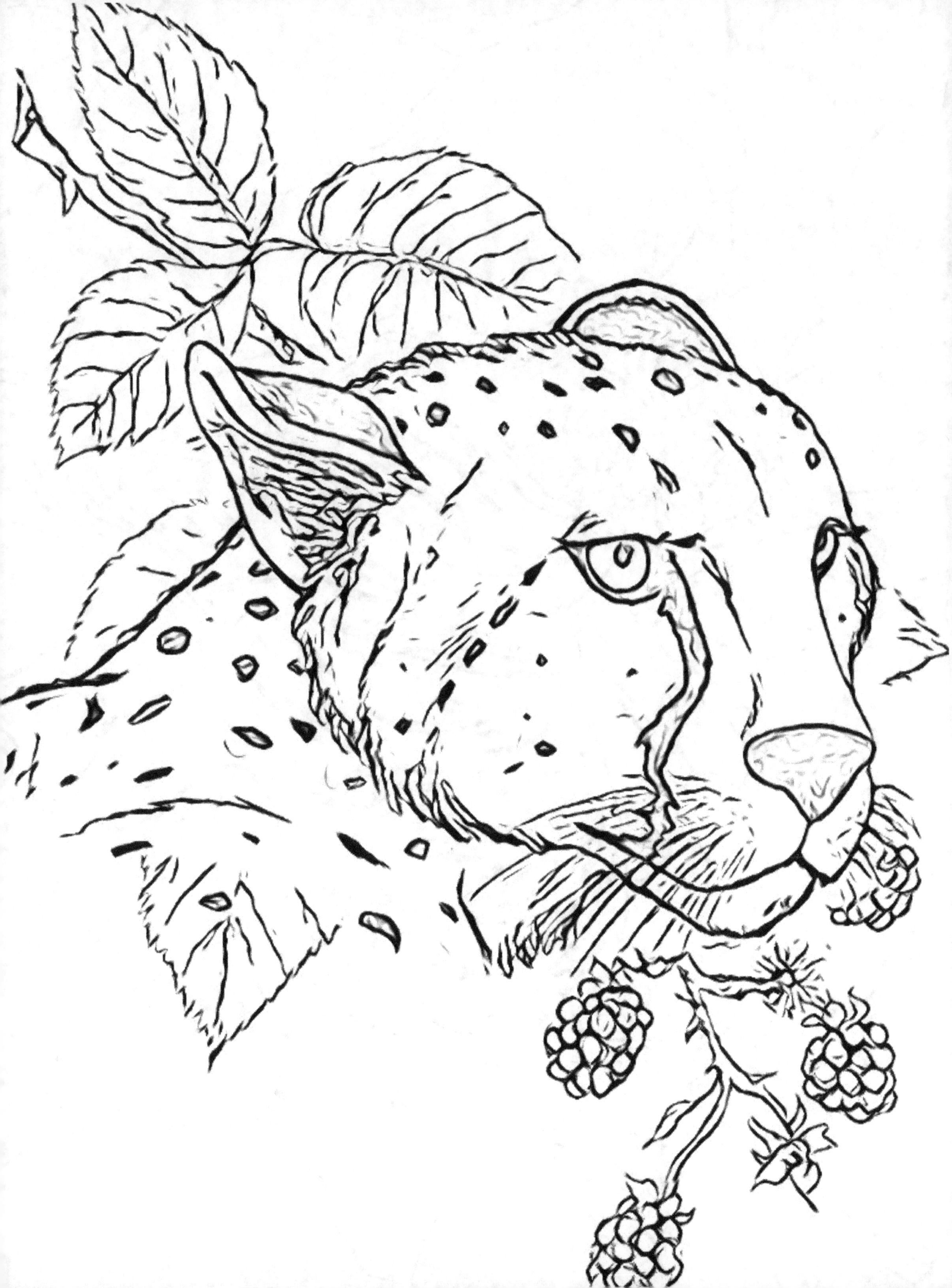

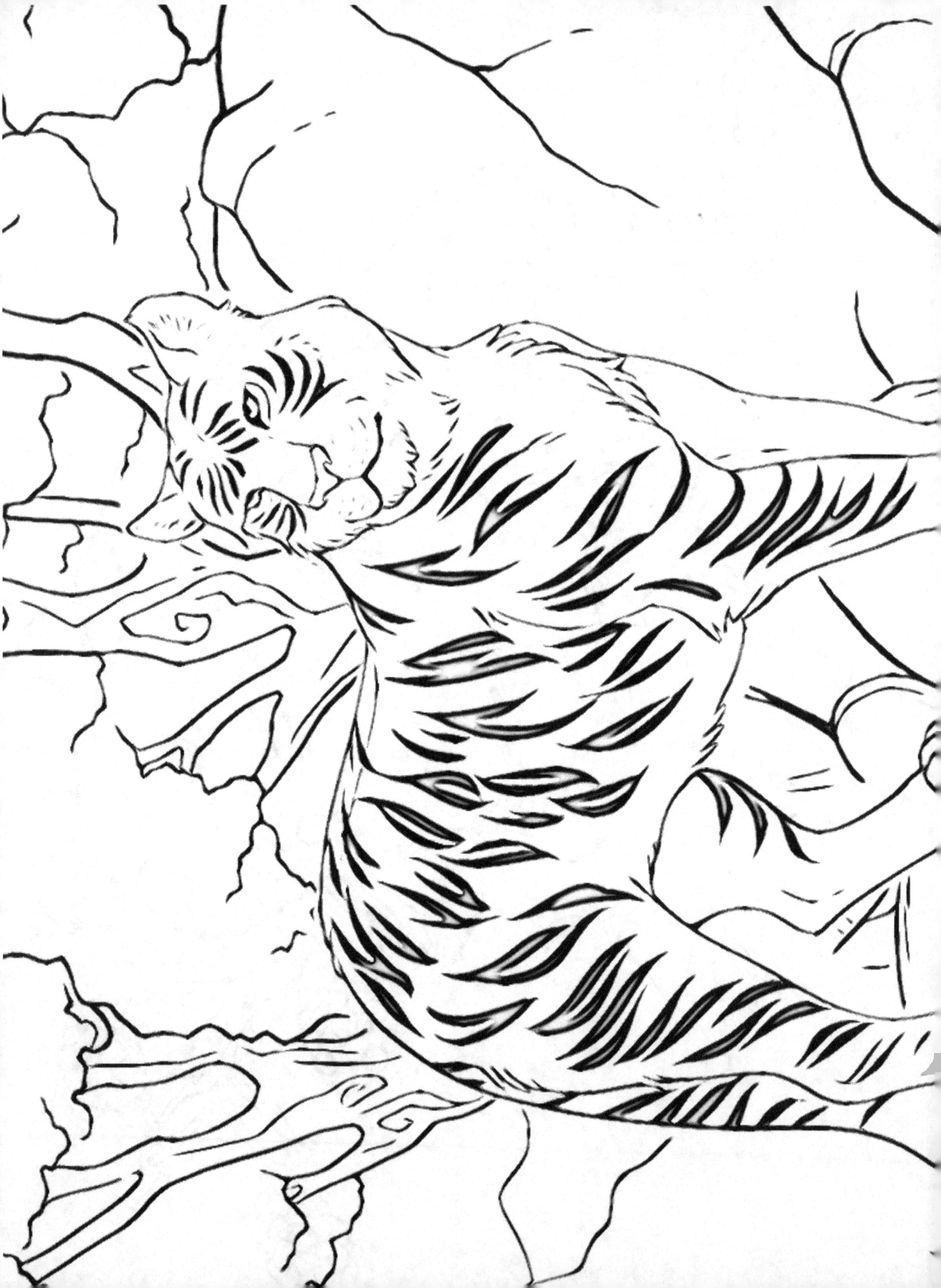

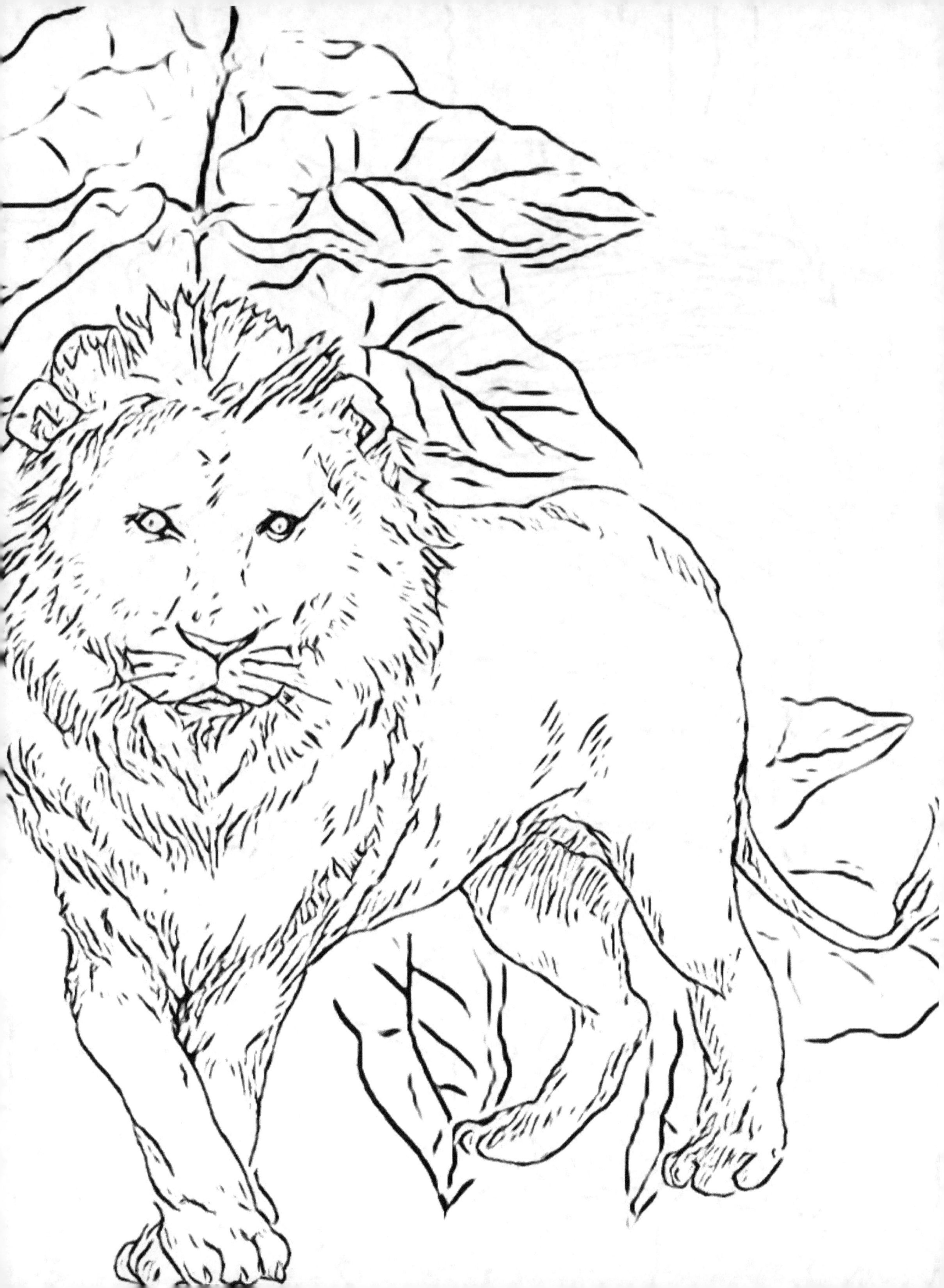

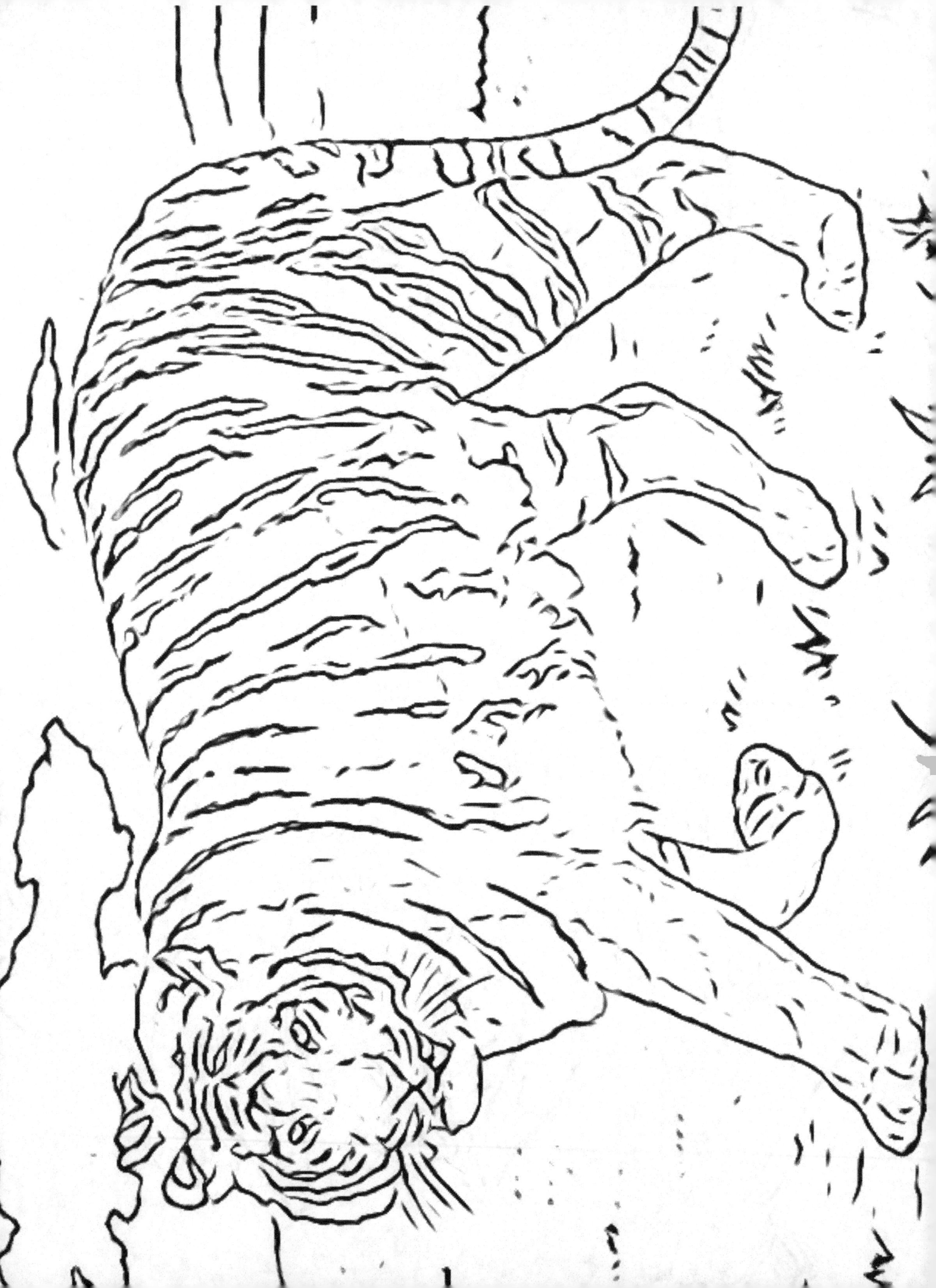

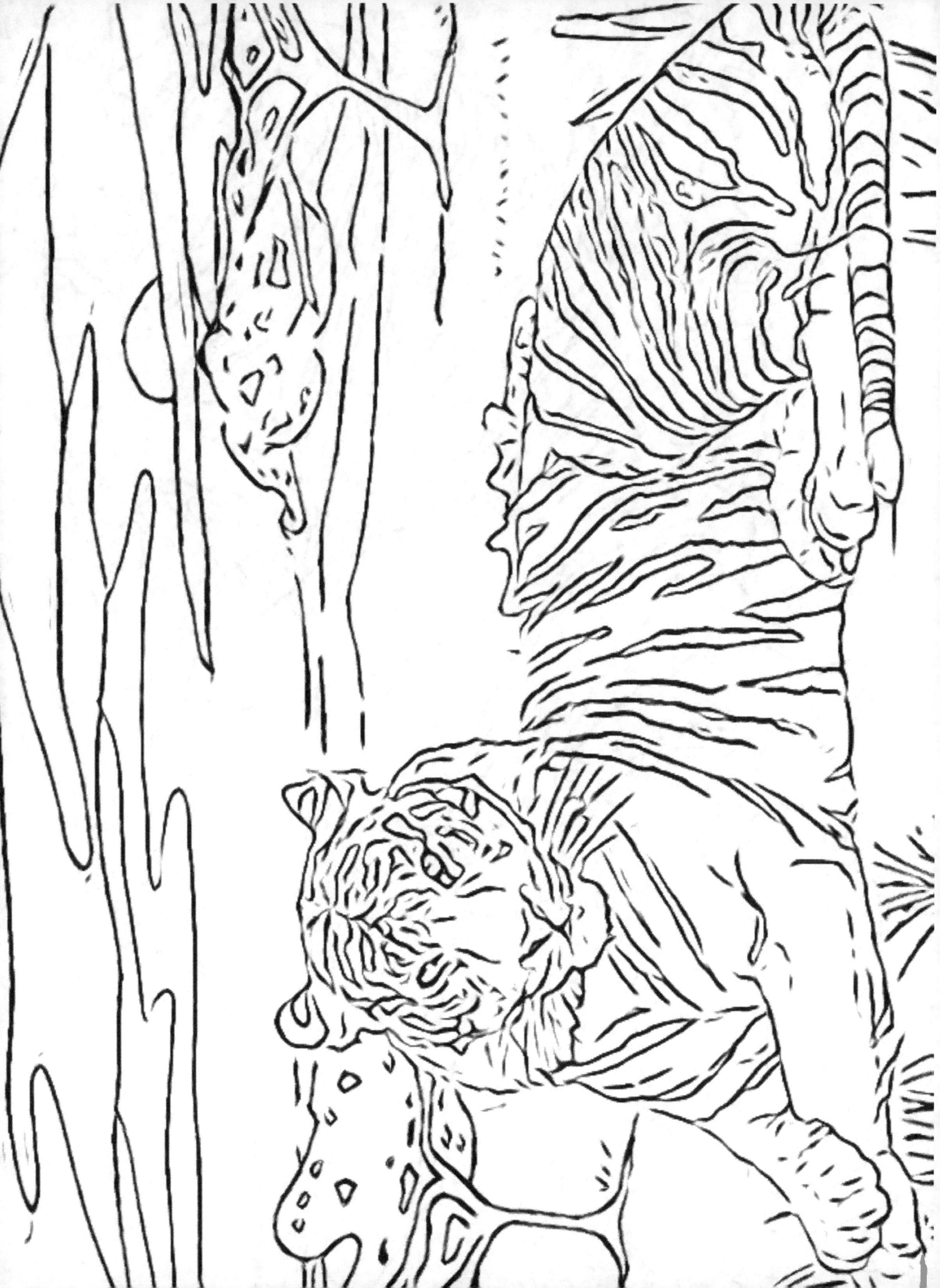

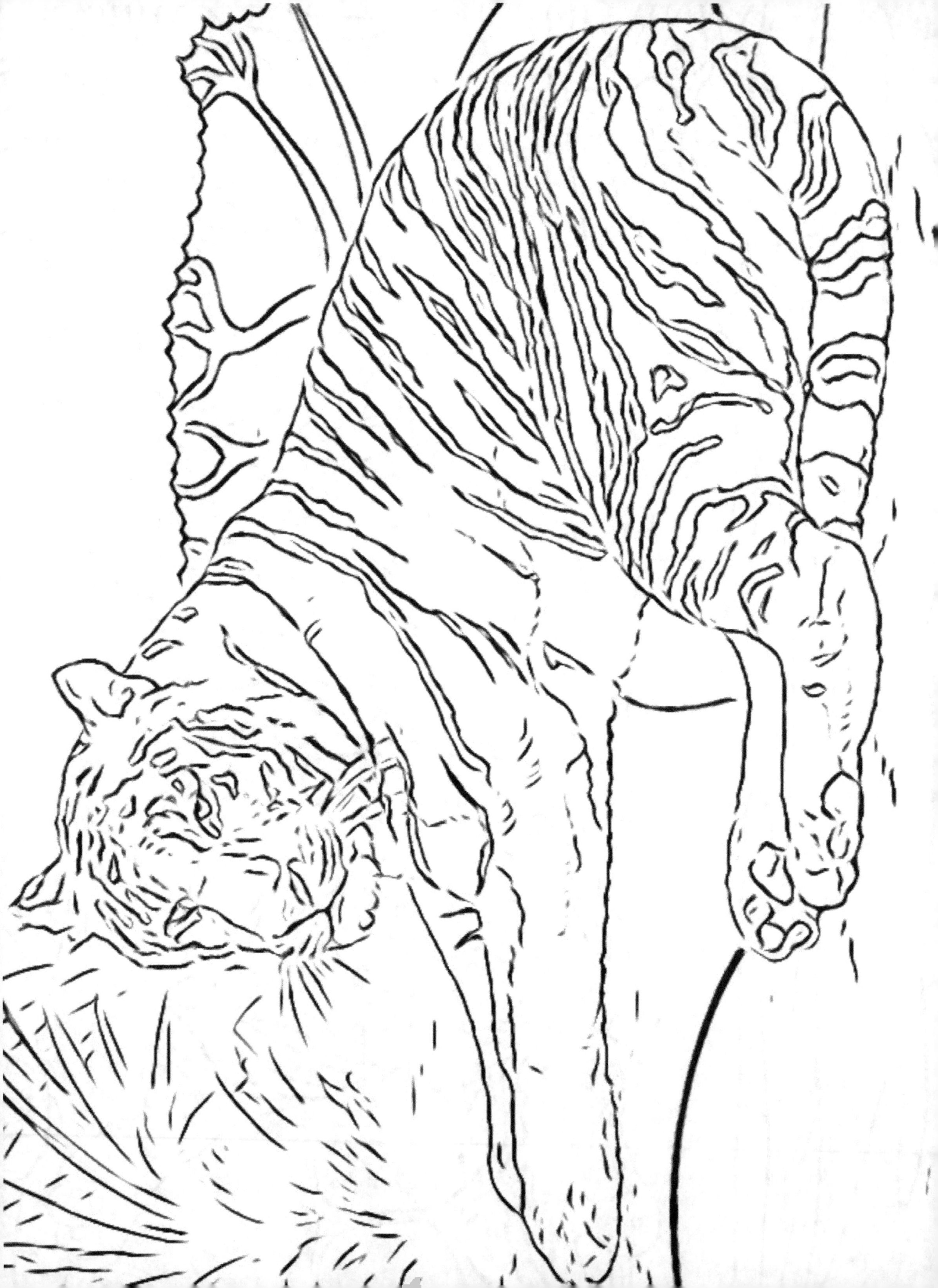

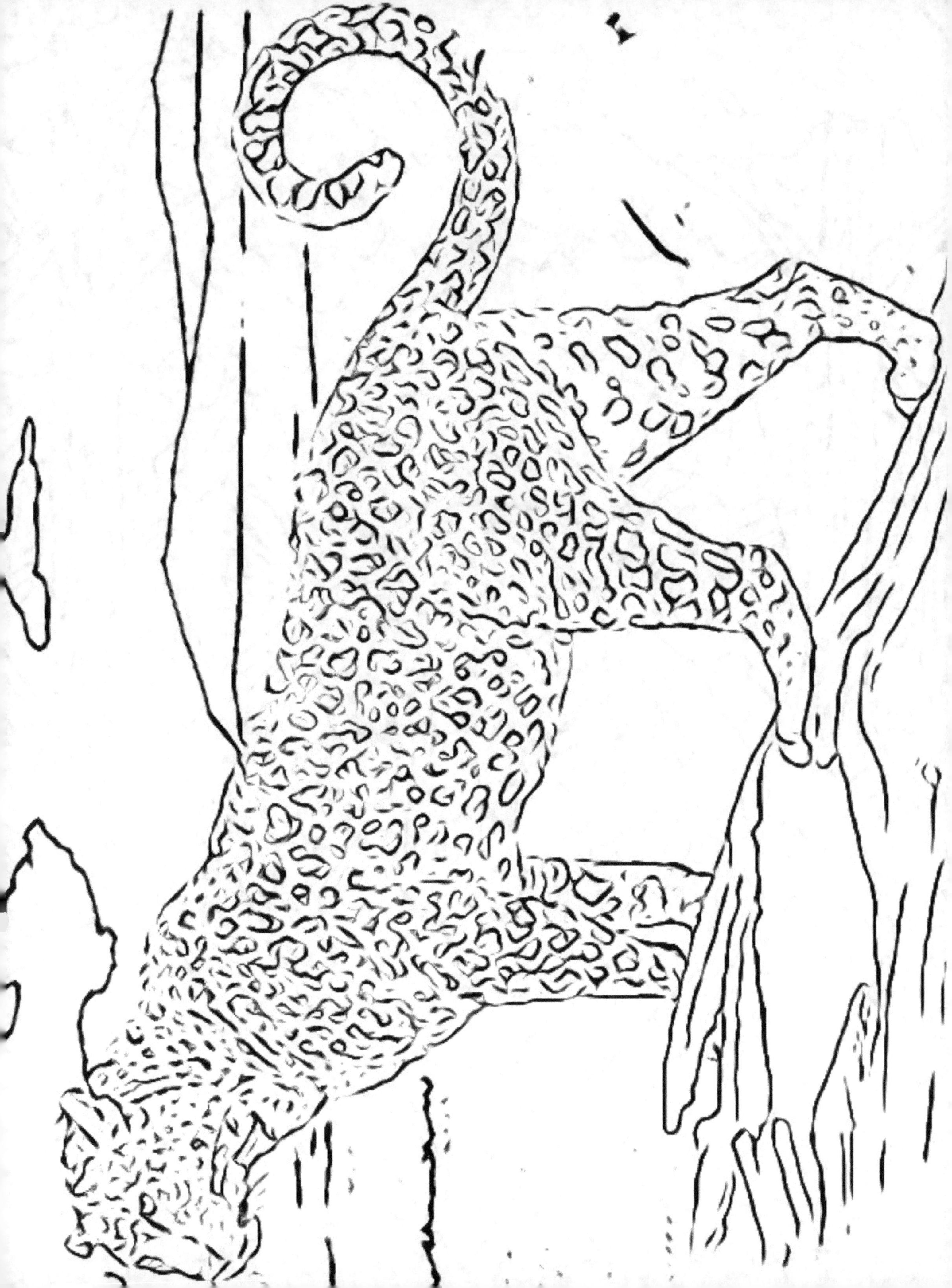

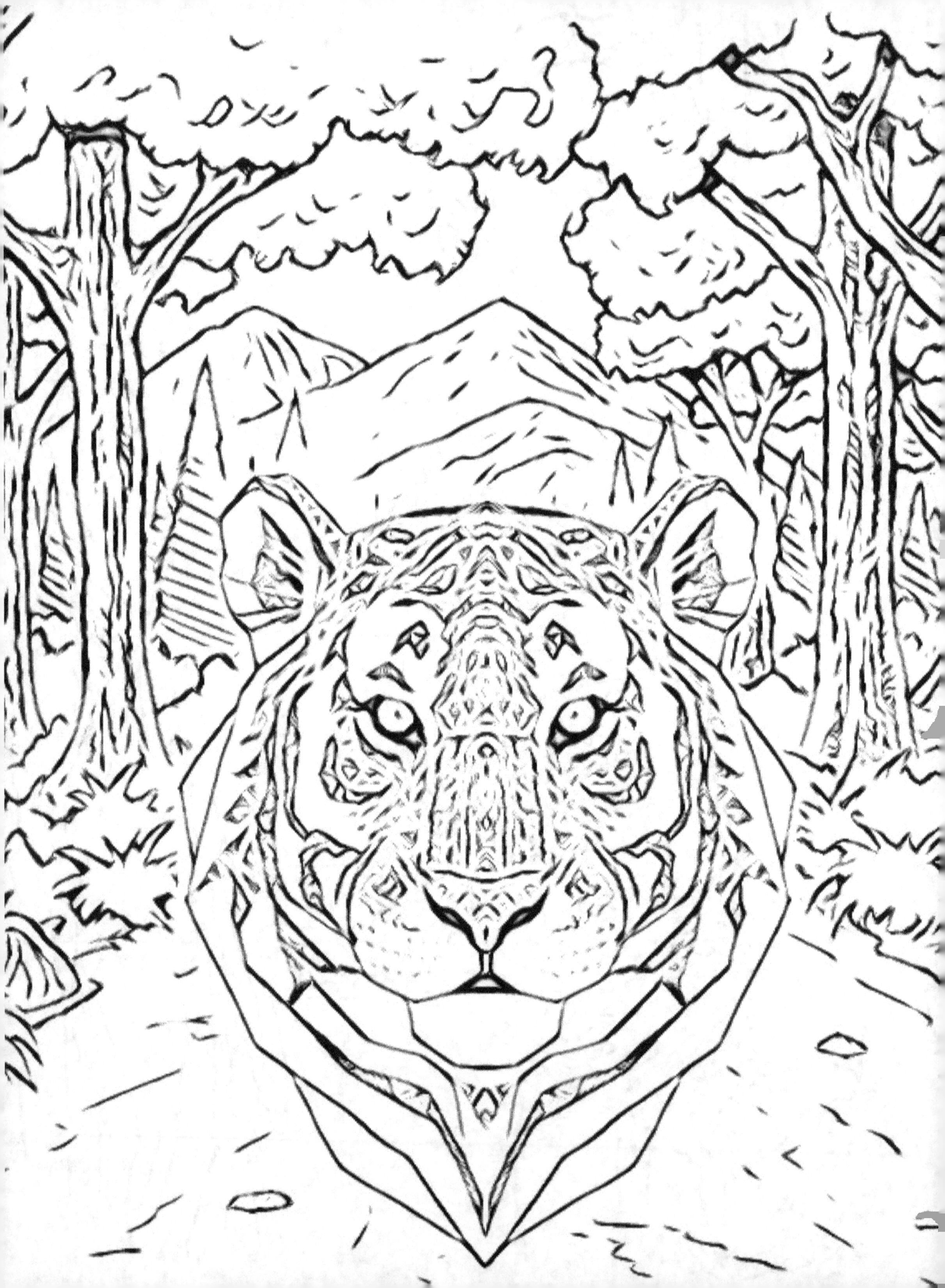

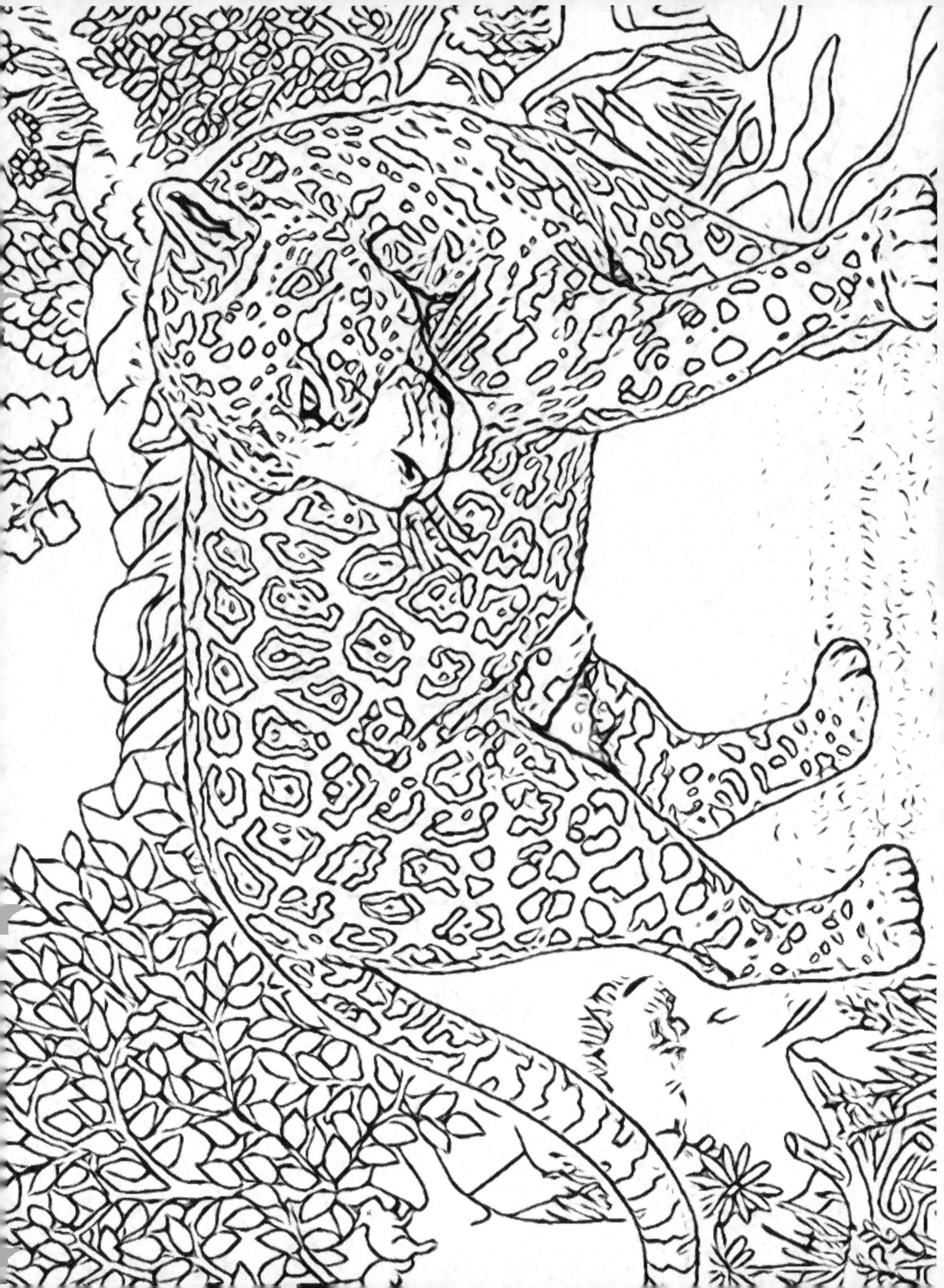

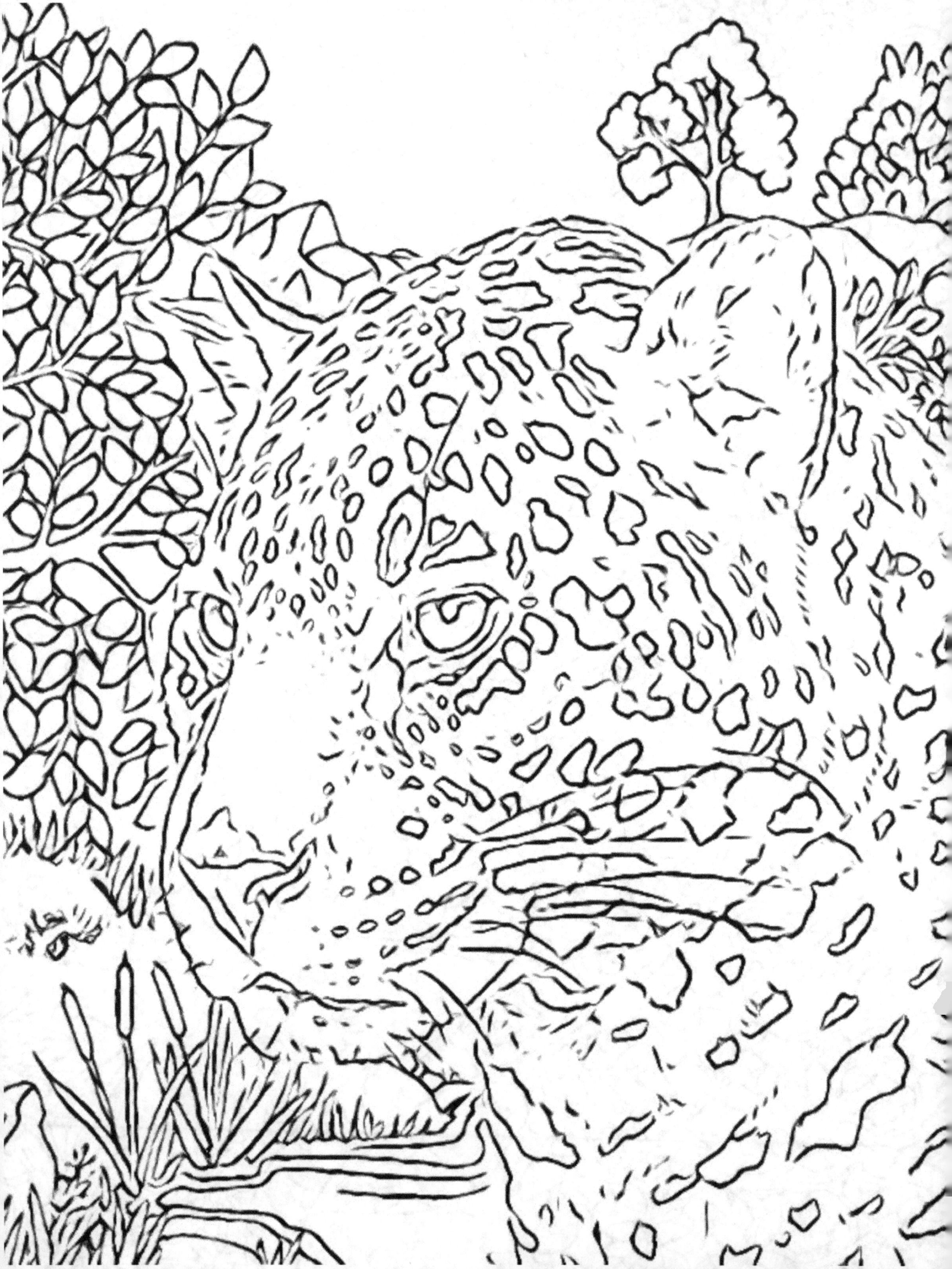

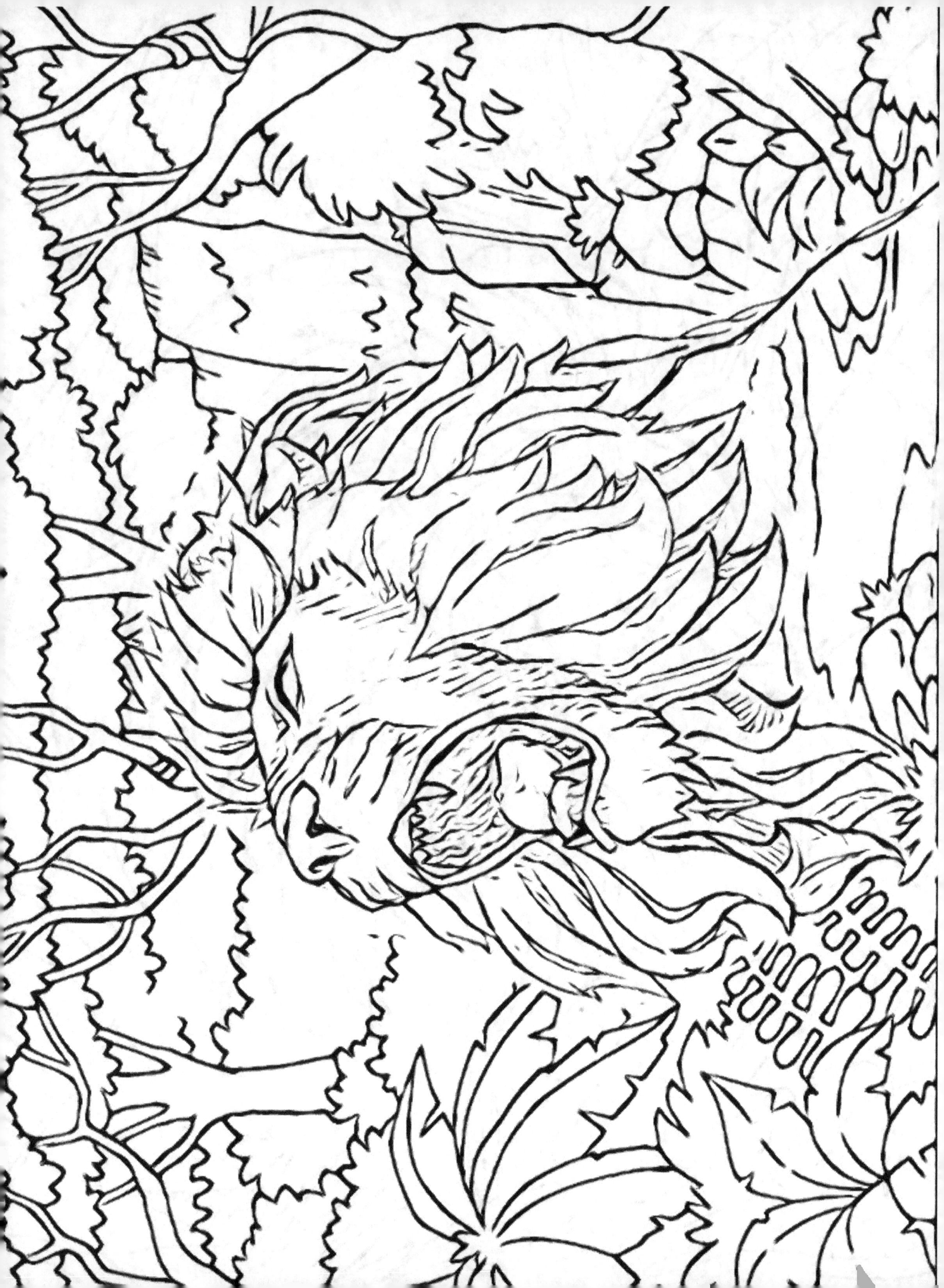

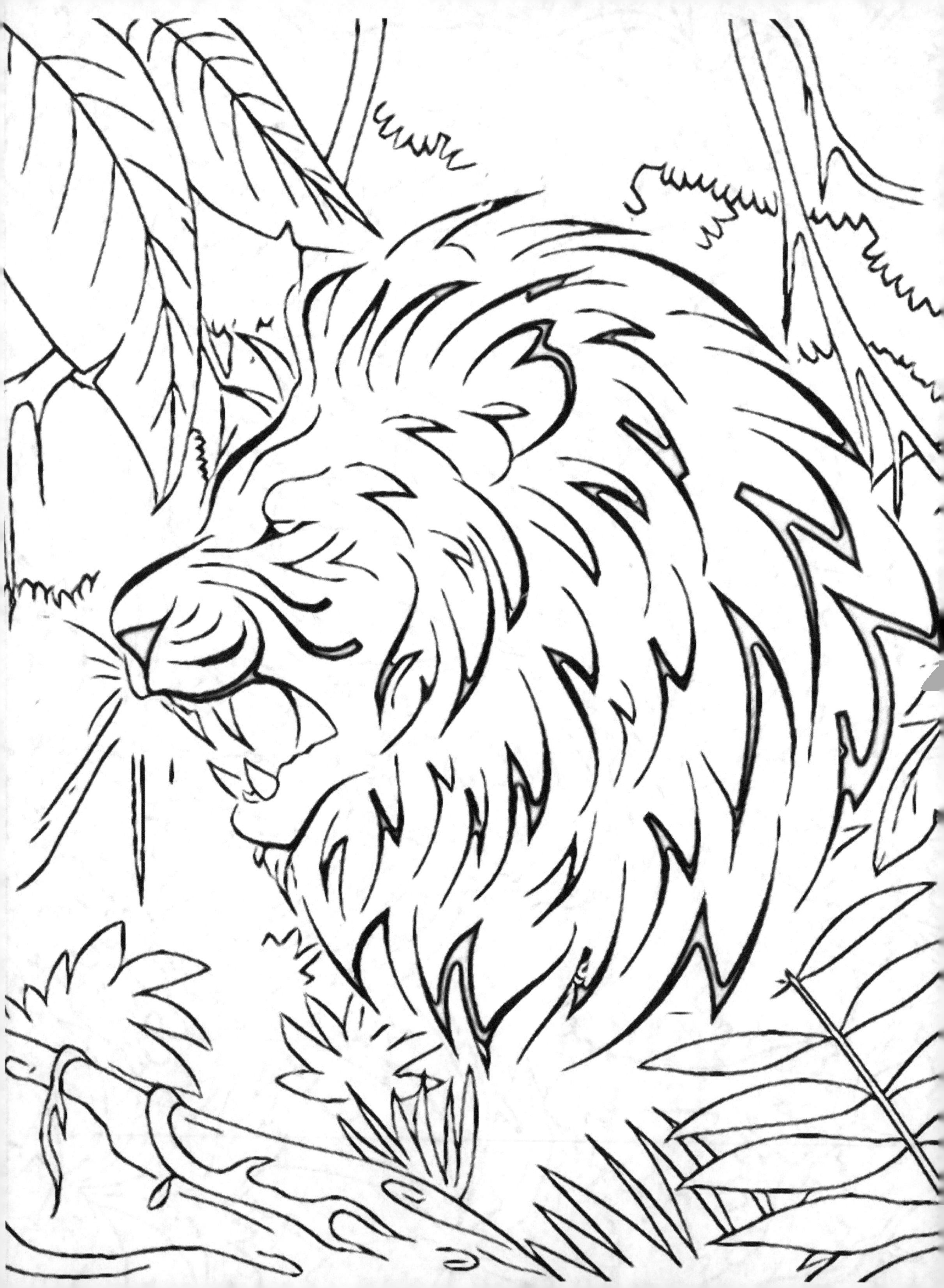

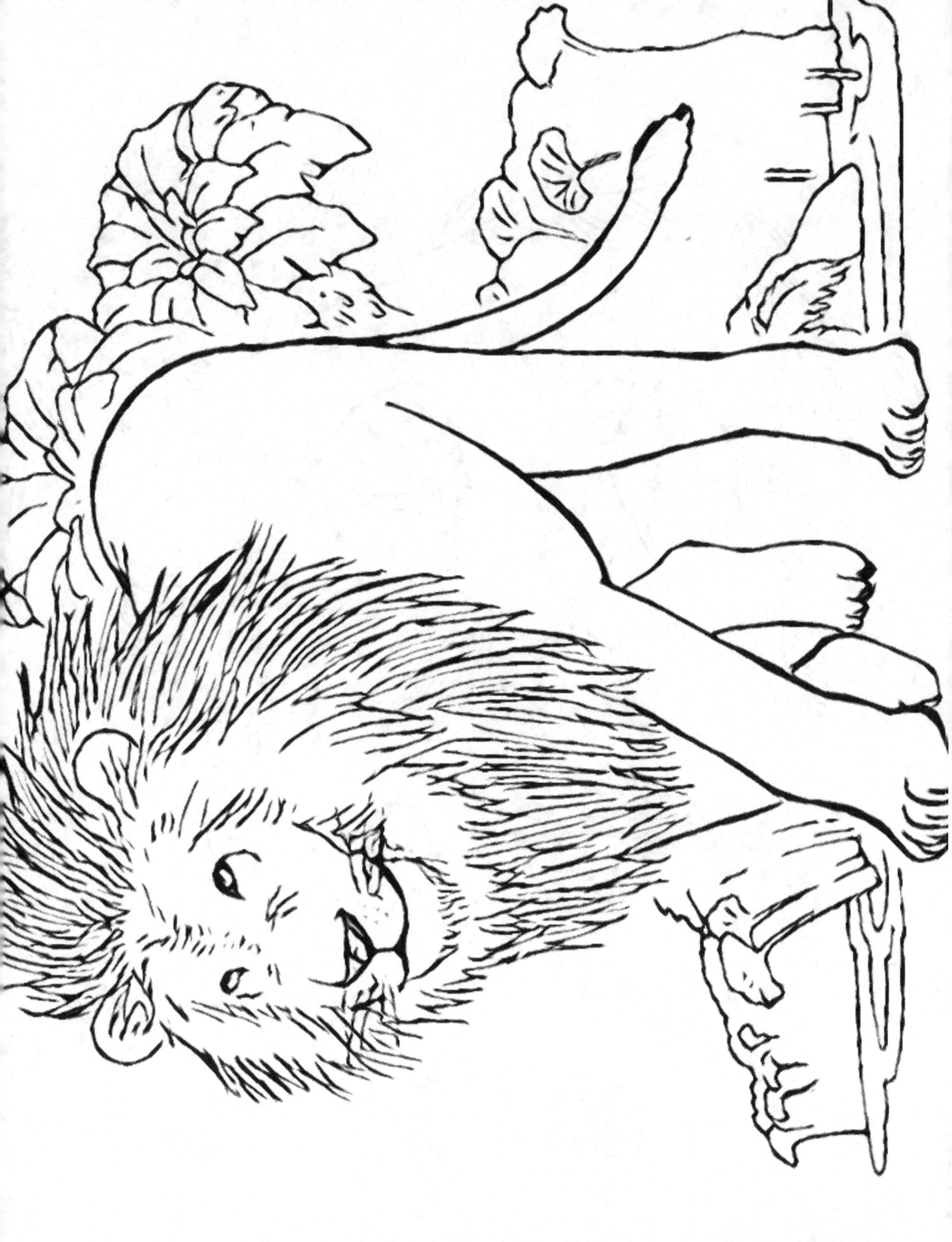

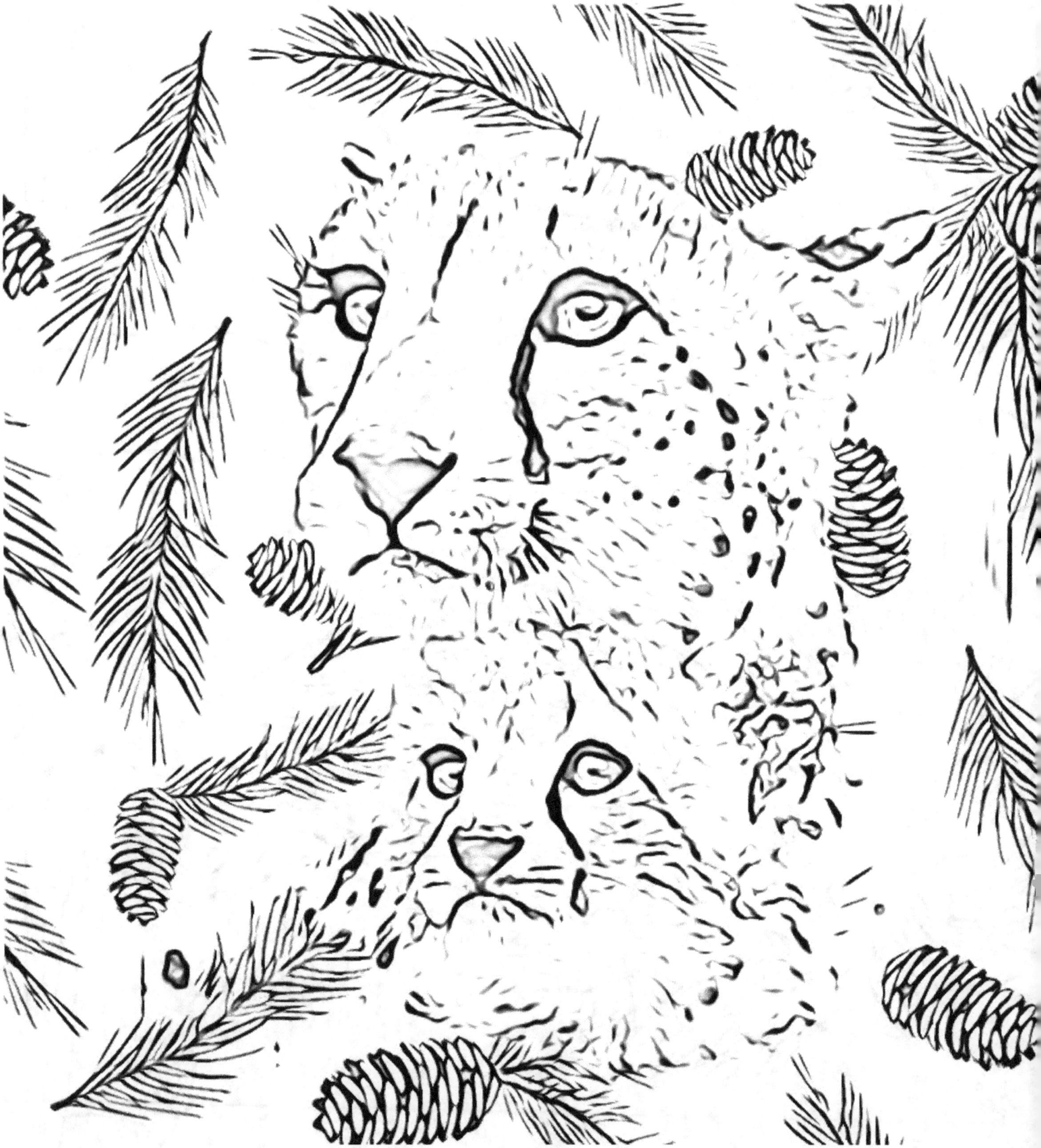

www.ingramcontent.com/pod-product-compliance
Lightning Source LLC
Chambersburg PA
CBHW081244170526
45165CB00009B/3191
* 9 7 8 1 3 8 7 6 8 6 9 6 4 *